13

SIMPLE

GREENHOUSE

GARDENING

SIMPLE
GREENHOUSE
GARDENING

Edited by

ALAN TOOGOOD

WARD LOCK LIMITED · LONDON

ACKNOWLEDGEMENTS

The publishers are grateful to the following for granting permission to reproduce the colour photographs: Harry Smith Horticultural Photographic Collection (pp. 2, 11, (top), 35, 39, 43, 51, 59, 63 & 71 (right)), and Pat Brindley (pp 11 (lower), 23, 50, 71 (left) & 79 (left)). The cover photograph was taken by Bob Challinor, courtesy of Arthur Billitt of Clack's Farm.

All the line drawings are by Nils Solberg.

© Ward Lock Limited 1987

First published in Great Britain in 1987
by Ward Lock Limited, 8 Clifford
Street, London W1X 1RB
An Egmont Company

House editor Denis Ingram

Text filmset in Bembo by
Paul Hicks Limited
Middleton, Manchester

Printed in Portugal

British Library Cataloguing in Publication Data
Simple greenhouse gardening.—2nd ed.
  1. Greenhouse gardening
  I. Toogood, Alan R.
  635'. 0483   SB 415

  ISBN 0-7063-6504-6

Frontispiece: The cool greenhouse need not be drab in winter and spring as daffodils and primulas are easily grown.

CONTENTS

PREFACE

Most books about greenhouse gardening assume from the outset that the reader is already an accomplished gardener, familiar with the techniques of gardening, and that he or she already possesses all the knowledge contained in its pages before reading the first chapter. The facts are often very different. This book, almost perversely, assumes that the reader knows practically nothing about greenhouses or gardening and progresses step by step through the stages of choosing a greenhouse, selecting a site, laying the foundations, putting it up, lighting it, heating it and maintaining it, and then goes on to describe the wealth of plants, fruits and vegetables that can be grown in the greenhouse, together with details of their temperature requirements and cultivation.

Simple Greenhouse Gardening contains, in simple lucid terms, all the information an amateur needs to run a greenhouse with the minimum of effort and maximum of pleasure and satisfaction.

A.T.

CHAPTER 1

GREENHOUSE STRUCTURE AND DESIGN

INTRODUCING THE GREENHOUSE

A greenhouse adds a new dimension to a garden. In it you can grow a range of exotic flowering plants, fruits and vegetables that would simply perish out-of-doors in the ill-mannered winters of a temperate climate. And it does not require a lot of time or expertise to get a great deal of fun out of a greenhouse.

Once you have a greenhouse, you can decide whether you are going to use it for growing exotic, tropical blooms, for forcing bulbs, raising cuttings, seedlings and summer bedding plants, or for growing tomatoes, melons, cucumbers, grapes and other luscious fruits and vegetables. However, since there is a relationship between the type of greenhouse you buy and the sort of crops you can cultivate in it, the first question to be considered is what type of greenhouse you want. There are two ways to tackle this problem: either work out what sort of plants you want to grow and select a greenhouse suitable for the purpose, or decide what you can afford and choose – as most people do – the best-value model in your price range.

Despite its mysterious reputation, greenhouse gardening is not difficult. There are no secrets to success. All you need to run a greenhouse that will give you the greatest pleasure for the least effort is to decide what you want to do, to find out the right way to do it, then do it.

A temperate climate, such as that of the British Isles, has many advantages to offer the outdoor gardener, but it also has its draw-backs: the majority of plants raised in the open have a growing season which lasts for little more than five of the twelve months of the year. Even then the bulk of outdoor flowers bloom in the first three months of the summer, while most of the fruit crop is produced in its last two months. Some garden plants, it is true, will flower in winter out-of-doors, but they are few in number, far from diverse, and the vagaries of the weather are such that they are not always very successful.

A greenhouse ameliorates the intemperance of the weather, and enables you to grow special plants. Just how special these plants may be depends precisely on the lengths you are prepared to go to in controlling the climate within the greenhouse. This in turn is largely determined by what you are prepared or are able to spend on the greenhouse itself and on heating it. Plainly, the greater the degree of control you wish to exercise over the greenhouse's internal atmosphere, the more it will cost you.

Basically there are four sorts of greenhouse to choose from, each maintained at a different temperature:

Cold greenhouses are heated solely by the sun. Although this restricts the house's usefulness to spring, summer and autumn, the results you get will depend a lot on where you live. Success will be greatest in sheltered, southerly spots, but even there the greenhouse will, except in abnormally mild winters, be useless for overwintering any plants which aren't hardy.

Cool greenhouses fit the needs and the pockets of many amateur gardeners. Unheated in summer, they are warmed artificially from autumn to spring to keep the temperature steady at about 7° C (45° F). Being frost-free the cool house is ideal for overwintering non-hardy plants like fuchsias and pelargoniums, dahlia tubers and other garden stock. During summer the greenhouse can be filled with crops like tomatoes that can be difficult to grow out-of-doors.

Intermediate houses have a minimum temperature of 10° C (50° F). This means that they will raise tomatoes, cucumbers and other crops, both winter and summer; are excellent for growing pot plants, and for propagation.

Warm houses, used for growing tropical plants, several kinds of orchids and for high-temperature propagation are heated so that they stay over 15.5° C (60° F).

Depending on the temperature, therefore, you will be able to grow a wide range of plants, shown in the table opposite. The cultivation of many of them is discussed in more detail in the second part of the book, but it is obvious that you do not, for example, need a warm house to grow orchids or even intermediate temperatures to be successful with melons and grapes.

COOL		INTERMEDIATE		WARM
Agapanthus	Marrow	Adiantum	Hyacinth	Aristolochia
Asparagus	Melon	Asplenium	Lettuce	Orchid
Azalea	Mint	Aubergine	Mustard and cress	Palms
Cacti	Orchid	Begonia	Nectarine	Pineapple
Chrysanthemum	Rhubarb	Bougainvillea	Orchid	
Cucumber	Sea kale	Carnation	Peach	
Cyclamen	Tomato	Chrysanthemum	Saintpaulia	
French bean	Vines	Cucumber	Strawberry	
Fuchsia		Freesia	Tomato	
Lettuce		Gloxinia		

CONSTRUCTION MATERIALS

Before you buy a greenhouse send off for all the brochures you can and read them thoroughly. You will then be in a good position to browse round a garden or greenhouse centre before making a final choice. Remember that the more glass there is in the greenhouse in relation to solid materials, especially when there are no brick or composition base walls, the more heat the house will lose when there is no sunshine. This means that it is more expensive to keep an 'all glass' greenhouse at the temperature you want than it is to keep a greenhouse with brick half-walls at the desired temperature (Fig. 1).

Fig. 1 Diagram showing how to calculate the area of glass through which heat is lost. Such calculations are necessary to find out how much heat needs to be put in the greenhouse to maintain any given minimum winter temperature.

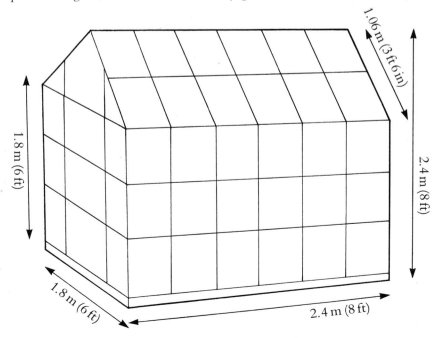

The majority of modern greenhouses are manufactured in prefabricated sections though there is nothing to prevent a do-it-yourself enthusiast from building from scratch. How easy they are to erect depends on the detailed design so it is well worth finding out in advance the time and trouble that will be involved in putting up a greenhouse of any particular type. The leading manufacturers deliver the complete greenhouse in sections anywhere in Britain and supply detailed erection instructions. When ordering a greenhouse, give the manufacturers clear, precise instructions.

Aluminium alloy, western red cedar (Fig. 2) and pressure-treated softwoods are the most common materials used for the framework of the greenhouse. Aluminium needs no maintenance. In aluminium greenhouses the glass is bedded on rubber or neoprene glazing strips and held in place with spring glazing clips. In timber houses glass can still be bedded on putty and held in place with glazing sprigs (headless nails), but a non-hardening sealing compound, which has a longer life, is more often used today. The table below sets out the main features of various greenhouse materials.

MATERIAL	STRENGTH/ BULK RATIO	COST	DURABILITY
Redwood	Medium	Low	Good if painted or treated
Steel	Very high	Low	Rusts unless galvanised or painted regularly
Pressure-treated softwoods	Variable	Low	Good
Red cedar	Low	Medium	Good
Aluminium alloy	High	Medium	Good
Imported hardwood	Medium	High	Good
Burma teak	High	High	Very good
Oak	High	High	Good

Light is all-important to plant growth and this is especially true of greenhouse plants, many of which come from very sunny climates. Because light is so vital take the trouble to ensure the best possible ratio between glass and framework in the greenhouse – but bear heating costs in mind.

GREENHOUSE SHAPE

The shape of your greenhouse will have an effect on the amount of light and heat reaching the plants within, particularly in Britain where the

Top Pendulous varieties of tuberous begonias are ideal for hanging baskets and flower freely throughout the summer.

Lower Coleus are raised from seeds sown in spring and provide foliage colour throughout the summer and into the autumn.

Fig. 2 A mini-sized greenhouse in red cedar.

angle at which the sun's rays strike the ground – the angle of incidence – varies widely from summer through to winter. Although in the north of the country the days are longer in summer, the angle of incidence is smaller and the sun's rays less powerful. The more acute the angle of incidence the less efficient your greenhouse will be, for the nearer the angle of incidence is to 90° the more light and heat will get into the greenhouse (Fig. 3).

A greenhouse with a conventional tent-shaped sloping roof will absorb light differently in different positions. If the length of the greenhouse runs east-west most of the sunlight in winter will be deflected off the roof and absorbed through the vertical side walls. Once the sun gets higher in the sky the south-facing slope of the roof will absorb radiation direct. Although sunlight will reach the back of the house this does mean that a dense crop of plants on the south side of the greenhouse will shade any plants behind.

GREENHOUSE TYPE	SPECIAL FEATURES	RANGE OF ACTIVITIES
SPAN-ROOFED (wood, alloy)	Brick base wall	Pot plants, propagation, chrysanthemums in pots.
	Weatherboard base wall	Retains less heat, but base wall can be lined with insulating materials such as fibre glass
	Glass to ground level	More costly to heat, but better light transmission makes them ideal for ground-grown crops.
LEAN-TO (Single pitch or ¾-span)	With or without base wall	Will grow most crops, but there can be problems with ventilation and overheating unless extractor fans are installed. Light distribution unequal. Excellent for peaches etc. against wall.
DUTCH LIGHT	Glass to ground level	Ideal for summer crops. Frequently used for lettuce and tomatoes. Much heat loss from loose glazing system.
CURVILINEAR	On small base wall or with glass to ground level	Both ideal for most activities. Heat loss fairly high with second type.
CIRCULAR	With or without base wall	Particularly good for pot plant culture and propagation. Fan ventilation is beneficial.
POLYTHENE TUNNEL	Tubular steel hoops clad with polythene	Ideal for vegetables

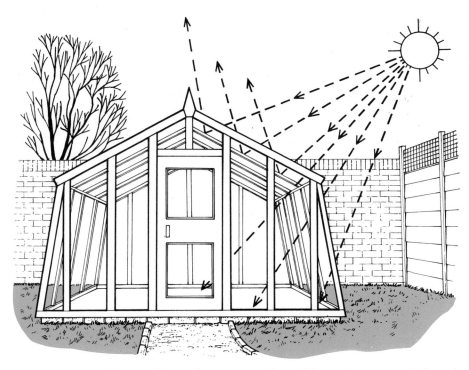

Fig. 3 Diagram showing how a large proportion of the sun's rays are deflected by the upper slope of a conventional span-roofed greenhouse.

Turning the greenhouse so that it faces north–south will even out the light in summer but has the disadvantage that in winter only the south-facing gable can catch the light. An east–west set-up will probably suit most gardeners best on balance, particularly if they use the greenhouse in winter, but it might be even more practical to select one of the greenhouse designs with a semi-circular curved roof (a curvilinear greenhouse) or one completely circular in shape. These greenhouses, the results of experiments to find the best design for absorbing winter sun, function well all the year round when lined up east–west.

Greenhouses are often classified according to the shape of their roofs:

Span-roofed houses, the most popular kind, are tent-shaped and have sides which are either vertical or slightly sloping. The roof rises to a ridge in the centre (Fig. 4). The angle of the roof varies widely. If you live in a place which gets a lot of snow in winter choose a more sloping roof. This will help avoid damage, especially if the house is unheated.

The size of a span-roofed greenhouse can vary from 1.8 × 1.2 m (6 ft × 4 ft) upwards, but the most popular size is 1.8 × 2.4 m (6 ft × 8 ft), as this leaves room inside for two 90 cm (36 in) benches and a 60 cm

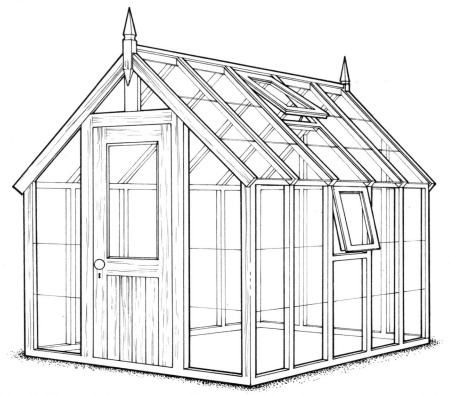

Fig. 4 The traditional span-roofed type. This is the most popular of all greenhouse designs. It has been tried and tested over a long period of time and can be relied upon to give good all-round performance.

(24 in) path or for two good-sized growing borders. The greenhouse glass can come right down to the level of the foundations or the vertical walls may be built up for 60–90 cm (2–3 ft) with brick or composition block. Or these base walls can be of wood. Some greenhouses have a base wall on one side and a glass front on the other, usually the south side, which is often an ideal compromise.

Gutters or eaves traverse the span-roofed greenhouse at between 1.2 and 1.8 m (4 and 6 ft), while the ridge itself is usually some 60–90 cm (2–3 ft) higher. The roof is fitted with ventilators and sometimes the sides, too, though these side vents are unnecessary if you decide to fit the greenhouse with an extractor fan. In this case ventilators need only serve as air inlets. Curved eaves represent a new departure from the traditional span roof shape.

Lean-to houses, unpopular in the past because they were difficult to ventilate, became overheated in summer and trapped little light in winter, are modern favourites (Fig. 5) because they are convenient to use and can be heated direct from the domestic heating circuit, particularly if house and greenhouse are built at the same time. New fan designs have solved the ventilation difficulties and the lean-to house can be very successful if situated facing south. If it faces west you might do best to use it as a conservatory to catch the evening sun, while a north-facing lean-to is ideal for growing ferns and shade-loving pot plants.

The roof of the lean-to can either be a single slope or a three-quarter pitch with a ridge. Unless you can use the extra height of a ridge to fit an additional ventilator above the top level of the back wall, and level with one on the opposite slope, it is probably not worth the extra expense. If you cannot afford extractor fans make sure the ventilators on sides and front of any lean-to give a good through-current of air. The construction of lean-to greenhouses is very similar to that of span-roofed shapes.

Porches, like lean-to greenhouses, can be very useful, particularly for growing pot plants. Their greatest disadvantage is that they tend to be draughty, so that plants are chilled as doors are constantly opened and shut.

Dutch light houses. Although greenhouses with glass reaching to ground level are sometimes called 'Dutch type', a true Dutch light

Fig. 5 Lean-to greenhouse. Greenhouses of this type are economical to run, since heating can often be taken off the domestic supply. They are ideal where one wants to grow a vine up the back wall.

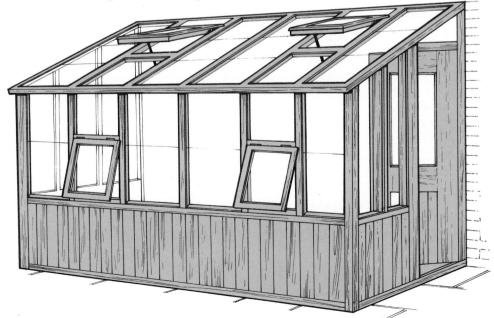

greenhouse consists of single sheets of glass, each framed lightly in wood and measuring 1.5 m × 75 cm (5 ft × 2½ ft), which are then bracketed together by their grooved sides. The gable ends are hinged so that they can be lifted to make room for a tall crop. Popular with lettuce, tomato and chrysanthemum growers, these greenhouses are not such a good proposition for an amateur because their all-glass composition means a large heat loss and because warmth is also lost from between the frames which have to be held loosely in place to prevent damage from the wind. But Dutch light greenhouses are comparatively cheap and easy to put up (Fig. 6).

An average single-span Dutch light greenhouse will measure 3.6–3.9 m (12–13 ft) in width and about 2.4 m (8 ft) in height. The low roof does restrict head and working room, but it is possible to build the whole house on to a brick base wall. One can buy aluminium- or timber-framed greenhouses of similar design to the Dutch light house and these do not lose quite so much heat.

Curvilinear or mansard houses, because they allow so much light to enter, make ideal all-purpose greenhouses. A house of this shape would be an excellent choice if you wanted to specialize in pot plants and propagation (Fig. 7). Made of alloy, they are extremely sturdy and obtainable in many different sizes and in lean-to form.

Fig. 6 Dutch type greenhouse. This type of greenhouse is best used for growing plants in borders inside the greenhouse, and is particularly useful for growing tomatoes, winter lettuces, many other vegetables and chrysanthemums.

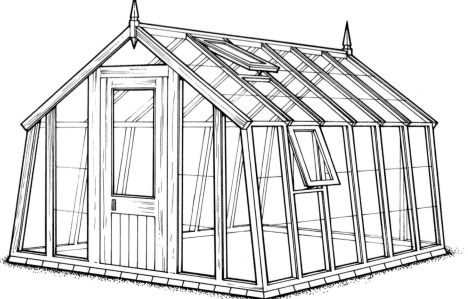

Geodesic or dome-shaped greenhouses are roomy and let in plenty of light. The panes of glass are triangular and there are usually solid panels at the base of the house. Available only with aluminium framework (Fig. 8). Looks superb in a modern setting and excellent for ornamental plant displays.

Circular houses are popular with small-garden owners (Fig. 9), but extractor fans are essential to prevent overheating in summer.

Polythene tunnels. The framework consists of galvanised tubular-steel hoops inserted in the ground. This is covered with a flexible polythene (or PVC) skin. Tunnels (Fig. 10) are far cheaper than other types of greenhouse and are excellent for growing vegetables. They are not usually heated as they quickly lose heat, though PVC retains heat slightly better than polythene. Generally there is a door at each end for ventilation although special tunnel ventilators are now available which are fixed to the cladding material. These help to solve the problem of excessive condensation. The polythene or PVC cladding has to be replaced every two to three years as it deteriorates and becomes brittle and discoloured.

Whatever their design, all greenhouses should be stable enough to

Fig. 7 Curvilinear greenhouse: glass panes at various angles.

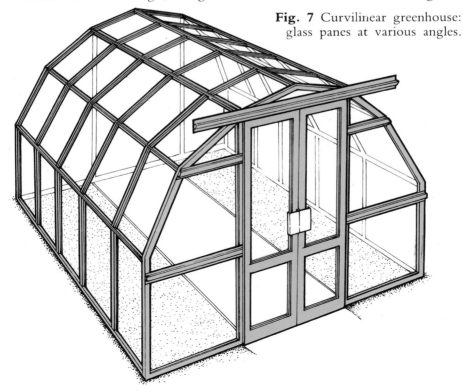

Fig. 8 Geodesic (dome-shaped) greenhouse (Solardome). Dome shaped greenhouses allow exceptionally good light transmission.

Fig. 9 Circular greenhouses are good to look at and useful for disabled gardeners who tend their plants from a wheelchair.

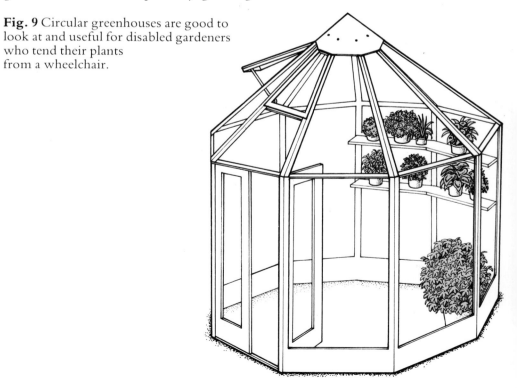

withstand really strong winds and constructed so that the panes of glass do not vibrate and shatter. When making your choice see that the greenhouse door is conveniently placed and wide enough to take a wheelbarrow and that it opens inwards or slides back and forth. Try not to buy a house so small that you always have to stoop when inside. Small houses can be raised by placing them on three courses of bricks.

SELECTING A SITE

The success of your greenhouse will depend a great deal on where you put it, for a convenient spot in the garden will be useless if it gets no sun. Your aim should be a position which receives the maximum amount of sunshine both summer and winter – but remember to take into account the shade cast by trees and buildings, and for the variation in the angle of incidence of the sun's rays from early summer to early winter.

A perfect greenhouse site will be well sheltered, but the shelter will not cut down the light. Shelter is important because it cuts down the risk of damage from storms; it also cuts down heat loss. You will probably have to compromise between the protection it gives and a loss of sun for a short time each day. In very exposed areas try to put the greenhouse between hedges running due north and south as this will give good exposure to the midday sun. Although you will lose some light in the morning and the evening the greenhouse will be sheltered from easterly and south-westerly gales.

Fig. 10 Polythene walk-in tunnel houses are cheap but not nearly so durable as their glass counterparts.

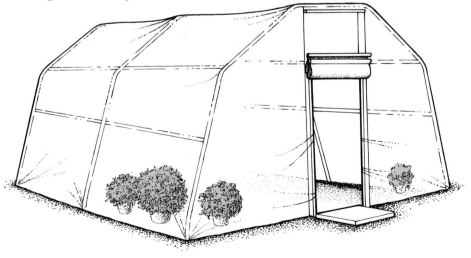

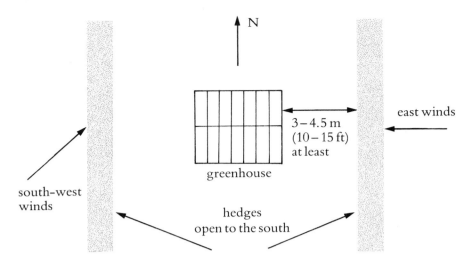

Fig. 11 Diagram showing the siting of the greenhouse in relation to the points of the compass, to prevailing winds and to shelter belts.

Keep the greenhouse at least 3–4.5 m (10–15 ft) from a hedge to avoid overshading and interference from root growth (Fig. 11). If trees are your shelter – like deciduous hedges they let light through in winter – double the distance. Solid walls are not a good idea: they stop the wind too sharply, deflecting it instead of breaking its force. Instead choose an open fence, plastic mesh or 'lattice' wall.

Three other vital factors in selecting a site for your greenhouse are water, drainage and electricity. A good supply of water near at hand is essential, but you will have to obtain official permission from the local water board to fit a permanent water supply from the house and be prepared to pay an increased water rate. If you decide on this system, lay the permanent pipe underground to prevent freezing. Although you may be able to lay plastic pipes yourself the job is probably best left to a qualified plumber.

Alternatives to a permanent pipe are the hose and the watering can, or an underground pipe fixed temporarily to an outside tap in, say, a garage. For the first of these methods, you will need a wide pipe, especially if you plan to use a spray or mist in the greenhouse as these need a good volume and pressure of water – about 18–27 kg per 2.5 cm^2 (40–60 lb per sq in). The second, temporary connection is tolerated by most water boards but does have the problem that water left in the pipes during winter may freeze and rupture the pipes.

Drainage is an aspect of greenhouse planning which is often ignored. A large amount of rain water will collect in the gutters or run off the roof of a greenhouse. If the greenhouse has gutters linked to vertical pipes connect these to a drain or to a seep hole, which is a gravel-filled drainage pit. Should the rain run straight on to the ground around the greenhouse lay tile or rubble drains joining up with a convenient field drain outlet or seep hole.

When planning your electricity supply look forward to the equipment you may acquire in future years. A light will use 100 watts of electric power, a heater 2½ kilowatts. Added to a soil-warming cable and possibly a mist irrigation unit, the total may be 4 or 5 kW., which will mean you will need a heavy-gauge electric cable. All electrical fittings and cable laying should be left to a qualified electrician, though you can do some of the preliminary work yourself.

Once you have laid your own greenhouse plans don't forget that you may need planning permission from your local authority. This planning permission is usually necessary for a greenhouse more than 1.8 × 2.4 m (6 ft × 8 ft), although regulations vary from area to area. To be on the safe side it is worth submitting a scale plan with the greenhouse position clearly marked in red, details of the dimensions (the manufacturer will supply plans, but you will have to draw these yourself if you are building your own greenhouse), and plans of the drains if they link up with main ducts. To support your application the written acceptance of landlord or neighbours is a good idea, along with any special aspects of your design such as attachment to the house.

A flat piece of land is the best place to start building a greenhouse but it is well worth making the effort to level sloping ground thoroughly, particularly if you want to use the top-soil to make borders inside the house. The easiest time to level is when the soil is dry and this will prevent damaging its texture. There are three methods:

Cut and fill. In this process the top-soil is stripped from the site and stacked on one side. The site is levelled by moving the sub-soil from the highest point to the lowest, then the top-soil is replaced. This simple procedure is excellent for a shallow slope but on steeper ground you will run into drainage problems unless you build a retaining wall with a drain behind it to collect water running down from the higher ground.

If the top-soil is deep you may not need to remove it, but whatever your method do not be impatient. Wait for the soil to subside before you lay the greenhouse foundations. It is usually best to leave the soil for a whole winter to settle.

Levelling to the lowest point involves stripping off the top-soil, stacking it, removing the sub-soil to the level you want, then putting back the top-soil. While it is simple this method can lead to drainage problems.

Levelling to the highest point is perhaps the best procedure, especially if the slope is acute, as it will solve most of your drainage difficulties. Use soil or ballast, depending on whether you want greenhouse borders, to raise the level. Add a wall at the base of the platform to keep the soil in place. The only disadvantage of this system is that drainage may be *too* efficient, with water running away too quickly because the greenhouse is largely above the normal soil level.

FOUNDATIONS AND ERECTION

The next step is to lay the greenhouse foundations but before doing this you will need accurate measurements of the greenhouse. To avoid frustration do wait until the greenhouse arrives, although delivery may take some weeks. Do not clutter up the site but ask for the sections to be off-loaded near by. Then check the plans carefully, make sure that all the parts that should have been delivered have, in fact, been delivered, and verify all the measurements, noting whether they are 'outside to outside', 'inside to inside' or 'centre to centre'.

Now peg out the exact position of the greenhouse. Rather than using odd pieces of cane take the trouble to cut 2.5 cm (1 in) square wooden pegs 35–40 cm (14–16 in) long and pointed at one end. Set one peg at the correct distance from fence, house or other landmark and then, using a good-quality steel measuring tape, put the other end peg in position, also at the right distance away from the landmark so that the greenhouse is in line. You can use a compass to check the orientation of the greenhouse.

To ensure accuracy measure from the centre of each peg and set the end pegs in exact positions, adding intermediate ones if the greenhouse is very long, kept in line by means of a tightly-stretched cord. For a small greenhouse a spirit level and a long straight board will be sufficient to check the horizontal level.

Now comes the task of setting the width of the greenhouse at exact right-angles to the length. The easiest way to do this is to make up an accurate triangle with pieces of wood, 1, 1.2 and 1.5 m (3, 4 and 5 ft) long, checking the right-angle formed with a joiner's square. Set the corner of this exactly to the nail and support the other two corners with bricks. Using two lines attached to the nail, form a right-angle along the edges of the triangle. Measure along the lines until you have the right width and insert stakes. Check that the lengthwise distance is still correct, level up all the pegs and tap a nail into the centre of each corner peg. If you have a builder's site square this will make really accurate right-angles, though you may need expert help to use it.

Tuberous begonias are the main providers of summer colour in many amateur greenhouses. Tubers can be kept from year to year.

Finally attach taut lines to the nails on each corner peg. This can be done by placing stout pegs 60–90 cm (2–3 ft) outside the outline of the greenhouse. Then remove the corner pegs. By doing this you will leave yourself plenty of room for manoeuvre and the foundations can be worked without detracting from your accurate start and without having to work round the pegs.

The greenhouse supplier will tell you what sort of foundations you need to support a base wall or base blocks. Laying foundations should prove no problem to the do-it-yourself expert but it is important to bear in mind that firm anchorage to the ground is essential.

Using the outside dimensions of the greenhouse as your guide, marked out with lines, dig a trench 12.5–15 cm (5–6 in) deep and 30–35 cm (12–14 in) wide if you are building a full 22 cm (9 in) width brick wall, 20–22 cm (8–9 in) wide if you plan a half-brick 11 cm wall or are using base or composition blocks. If you have just levelled the soil you may need to dig deeper to find undisturbed ground.

Mix the concrete for the foundations using three parts aggregate, two parts rough sand and one part cement. Run this in as a layer at least

Fig. 12 A sequence showing construction of a timber greenhouse from beginning to end. Note that a level site is needed before construction can begin.

d

e

f

10–12.5 cm (4–5 in) deep and use a straight board to make it level. According to the maker's directions, set in any necessary securing bolts at this stage. Once the foundations have hardened you can begin building up bricks or blocks, using a three to one mixture of sand and cement (measured by bulk). Stick closely to the plans so that the base wall keeps to the exact greenhouse dimensions. As the walls rise do not forget to leave spaces for doors and ventilators. Check the vertical truth of the walls frequently using a spirit level and plumb line. If the base wall is very high, or your site slopes slightly, you may need to reinforce it by hammering in sharpened piles.

The final part of the building will depend on your style of greenhouse but full instructions are usually supplied. Large modern prefabricated sections should present few difficulties (Fig. 12).

MAINTENANCE

Although modern greenhouses need minimum attention there are some chores you cannot avoid. Wooden greenhouses made of hardwoods like oak and teak need little or no treatment to keep them in good condition, though they may well benefit from an occasion oiling with linseed. Red cedar can be left untreated, in which case it will mellow to silver-grey, or it can be treated with a cedar perservative, obtainable from the makers or from garden centres. If pressure-treated in advance softwoods will last for a long time without painting, though they are not very attractive.

Untreated softwoods will need regular painting to prevent weather damage. Either use white paint on top of a priming coat and undercoat, or, if the wood can be cleaned with a wire brush, apply aluminium paint. If putty has been used for glazing, paint over it and add 3 mm (⅛ in) of paintwork over the glass to give a good seal. Use masking tape to achieve a clean straight line.

Painting both the outside and the inside of a greenhouse definitely increases the amount of light reflected into it. As an alternative you can treat wood with a horticultural wood preservative but the job is best done before the house is erected. It costs very little to have wood pressure-treated before you buy the greenhouse and this is even more effective. Alloy houses need no painting but steel hoops of tunnels may eventually need painting with aluminium-based paint.

Even if you plan to paint them eventually, treat benches and shelves first with horticultural wood preservative. Because it gives off da-maging fumes, especially when heated, *never* use creosote for this job.

Dirt is the great enemy of the greenhouse gardener. In towns and cities in particular it sticks to the glass, both inside and out and cuts down the amount of light passing through the glass. Cleaning the glass does not take very long. For the outside use a proprietary glass cleaner. Spray it on the glass and wash it off with the hose pipe. To clean the inside any good detergent will do but remove the plants before you begin. Use a scraper to get rid of moss and algae growing over the glass and wash them away with a jet of water. Or use a horticultural algicide.

Once a year give the inside of the base walls a good scrub and paint them with white masonry paint. Give any heating pipes an occasional coat of aluminium paint. Contrary to popular belief this will not impair their heating performance.

HEATING A GREENHOUSE

Heating an ordinary house and heating a greenhouse have much in common yet it is easy to become confused because of all the talk about the efficiency of different methods.

Any heating engineer worthy of his name will start an appraisal of a heating project by calculating the heat loss of a building. The first figures to know are those for the heat-moving, and thus the heat-losing powers of various materials. Known as the *thermal conductivities* of substances, these powers are measured in standard British Thermal Units (BTUs) and universally accepted as follows:

Material	Heat conducted per sq ft per hour for every degree F.
Glass (including its framework)	1.1 BTU per hour
4½ in brick or composition block	0.5 BTU per hour
Double brick wall, 9 in thick	0.4 BTU per hour
Wood 1 in thick	0.5 BTU per hour
Concrete 4 in thick	0.75 BTU per hour
Double glazed glass (properly sealed)	0.5 BTU per hour

This table shows that glass loses heat more than twice as fast as wood or brick and that double glazing cuts heat loss by half. Technically speaking heat is also lost through the floor but this is usually ignored as the ground area of the greenhouse often stores heat very effectively then throws it back into the greenhouse.

To calculate the heat loss of your own greenhouse you must measure the total areas of glass and brick, cement or wood in square feet, and multiply each by the above figure for the thermal conductivity. The plan sheets are easiest to use for this.

The heat lost by a perfectly tight 1.8 × 2.4 m (6 × 8 ft) glass to ground greenhouse is 259 BTUs per hour. But an average greenhouse is bound to have some leaks. A very exposed greenhouse will lose more heat than the norm, a sheltered one less. A realistic addition to the heat loss is a third of the normal, giving here a figure of 343 BTUs.

Having made your calculation, you must now decide how much you want to heat the greenhouse. This will depend on where you live and what you want to grow. A greenhouse kept at 15.5° C (60° F) in all weathers will need a 'lift' of some 20° C (40° F) over the outside temperature, assuming that this may drop as low as −6.5° C (20° F). To work out the heat input simply multiply the heat loss, in this case 343 BTUs, by 40. For an intermediate house multiply by 30, for a cool house by 25. As a sample calculation, 343 × 30 gives 10,290. This is the number of BTUs needed to heat the intermediate greenhouse, whatever your heat supply.

But these calculations represent the ideal. In practice there are several factors which can influence your heat equation. The most important of these concerns the properties of glass, for while glass is a first-rate transmitter of heat and the heat of the sun passes through it with ease, it is, at the same time, a poor insulator. This means that while glass can trap a large spectrum of the sun's heat waves, it cannot store heat for long. Once the temperature outside the greenhouse drops, glass will quickly transmit the heat back again.

Reducing the area of glass in your greenhouse will cut down this heat loss but a great deal of warmth will be sacrificed unnecessarily if your greenhouse has badly-fitting doors and ventilators or is poorly glazed. A high wind outside the house will step up the heat loss even further.

Double glazing is effective in reducing wasted heat because it traps a pocket of insulating air between two layers of sealed glass. Although costly, double-glazed greenhouses are on the market but an alternative, albeit a rather crude one, is to line your greenhouse internally with bubble polythene. If you do this remember to leave the ventilators free and bear in mind that you may need to fit extractor fans to cope with the increased condensation.

In Britain's changeable climate artificial heating is the only way of keeping a greenhouse at a reasonable temperature all the year round. The amount your heating will cost will depend on the fuel you choose, on the sophistication of the system – it could be automatic or semi-automatic to save you work and worry – and the efficiency of the heat-producing units. All systems waste some heat, usually through the flue pipes, but any reputable supplier will give you an accurate estimate of total costs.

There are four main methods of heating a greenhouse:

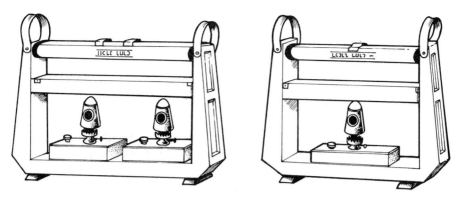

Fig. 13 Typical paraffin heaters for greenhouses. Such heaters are safe to use, economical to run and some can be controlled by a thermostat.

Hot pipes. These contain hot water which is, in turn, heated by a boiler fired by solid fuel, oil or gas. The simplest solid-fuel boilers will need daily stoking, but some solid-fuel systems are semi-automatic. If you choose a new gas, oil or electric boiler then it will work on a completely automatic electric-powered time-switch.

Oil heaters can either be simple paraffin stoves which heat the air in the greenhouse direct (Fig. 13), or consist of more complicated pressure jet or vaporized burners which for instance heat air in ducts, possibly with the assistance of fans. Electricity is needed to work these fans and the pressure jet burners and can be used to control a thermostat system. Unsophisticated oil heaters must be regulated by hand.

Gas heaters can be powered by natural gas or bottled gas. They consist basically of a warm-air cabinet and are thermostatically controlled. Natural-gas heaters are cheaper to run than those which work off bottled gas, but you first need a gas supply to the greenhouse. This can be expensive to lay on and the system will have to be installed by a professional gas engineer.

Electrical heating systems come in five different designs, each ideal for automatic control:

1. *Soil or bench warming cables* heat the growing medium, but have little effect on the air temperature inside the greenhouse.
2. *Air-warming cables* are installed round the walls of the greenhouse and held in place by porcelain clips.
3. *Tubular heaters* (Fig. 14) come in many shapes and sizes and are best fitted to the greenhouse walls.
4. *Fan heaters* (Fig. 15) can be placed anywhere but work best in the

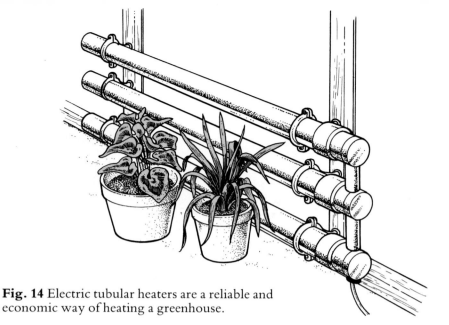

Fig. 14 Electric tubular heaters are a reliable and economic way of heating a greenhouse.

centre of the house. The largest fan heaters, however, are placed at one end of the greenhouse and hot air is distributed through perforated polythene pipes.

5. *Convection heaters* can be placed anywhere in the greenhouse.

TYPE OF SYSTEM	AVERAGE OPERATIONAL EFFICIENCY
Solid fuel boiler, simple design. Hard coal.	50%
More refined solid fuel boiler using smokeless fuel or coke	60%
Purpose-made oil-fired boiler and fan heaters with external flue (some types have no flue and this results in slightly higher operational efficiency)	75%
Converted oil-fired boiler with vaporizer type burner (Figure for free-standing oil heaters is similar)	70%
Purpose-made gas-fired boiler	75–80%
All types of electrical heaters	100%

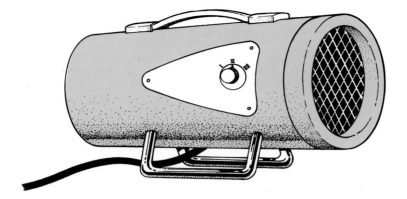

Fig. 15 A through-flow type electric greenhouse heater. Such heaters have the advantages of keeping the air in the greenhouse circulating and of ensuring that all parts are heated properly.

Once you have produced a high temperature inside your greenhouse the next problem will be to distribute it evenly, particularly in cold weather. Hot water pipes are the best by far. Transmitting heat by the convection currents of rising hot air, they can set up a warm curtain of air around the greenhouse. And by the process of radiation they warm the soil, a special bonus for heat-loving crops like tomatoes. Benches, too, will benefit from hot water pipes, but the pipes will only work efficiently if kept at the same temperature all along their length. Place the pipes round the edges of the greenhouse.

A heater which merely pumps out warm air from one spot is not ideal, especially in a freezing snap or when one side of the greenhouse is exposed to a prevailing cold wind. These heaters, which work entirely through convection, will be far more useful if they can be fitted to fans or, even better, to a network of perforated polythene pipes to push the air out evenly. But whatever your choice do not hesitate to seek the advice of a heating expert.

When selecting pipes to carry hot water, decide on the modern 3 cm (1¼ in) diameter rather than the old 10 cm (4 in) system. Although you will need a greater length of the small-bore pipe, and it will cool down quickly, it will save you money because there is much less water to heat. Narrow pipes will give you much better control over the greenhouse temperature as they respond quickly to the thermostat.

If you plan to install a very large footage of small-bore pipe there may be some problems when it comes to water circulation, so budget for a circulating pump. If the difference in temperature between the water in the pipes and the air in the greenhouse is 38° C (100° F) the amount of heat given off by them, per foot, will be:

DIAMETER	HEAT EMITTED (to nearest round figure)	DIAMETER	HEAT EMITTED (to nearest round figure)
1 in	80 BTU	2½ in	150 BTU
1¼ in	100 BTU	3 in	190 BTU
1½ in	110 BTU	3½ in	200 BTU
2 in	130 BTU	4 in	230 BTU

To work out how much piping you will need, divide the figure above into the total heat load for the greenhouse which you worked out before.

On the whole, pipe systems, whatever the heating method, are most economical to run, but much depends on the cost of the fuel and they are more expensive to install. The cheapest sort of oil-burner – rather than oil stove – is a vaporizing one which is installed in a steel or cast-iron jacket. Rely on expert installation if you choose this system. Unless the flame and the draught are carefully regulated much of the gas produced will be wasted.

Always put the boiler on the side of the greenhouse which is sheltered from the prevailing winds. This will stop flue gases from staining the glass. If you can, put the boiler outside the house, on the north side – it will work more efficiently, be protected from the wind and emit a steadier draught.

The advice of a supplier is a must before installing a pipe system. The final layout will depend on the pipe diameter you choose and on whether you add a pump to assist the circulation. In general pipes work best on the so-called *thermo-syphon principle*. The pipes rise 2.5 cm (1 in) every 3 m (10 ft), and at the highest point in the system there is a tank or valve. The temperature in the pipes is kept constant because hot water rises, is cooled and falls to the bottom of the system. A drainage point – fixed on the boiler or return pipe – is vital. From it, the pipes can be drained when not in use during cold weather, to prevent cracking, a procedure which is *all important*.

Modern circulating pumps largely do away with the need for a thermo-syphon system, which means that pipe layouts can be much more flexible. Pipes can be put where they fit most conveniently and flexible rubber couplings can be used instead of metal ones. They can be used under benches for propagation, then dropped to ground level when the benches are removed to plant, for example, a crop of tomatoes. This particular versatility is especially useful for providing heat for warmth-loving crops.

Control is simplicity itself if you have an electrically-operated system, for it can be linked up to a thermostat which gives a high degree of control. Constant attention, however, is the only secret of success with a simple oil-fired stove. Solid-fuel boilers, too, need much care if they are to keep the greenhouse temperature even, but today's gas and oil pipe systems are self-regulating from a thermostat within the greenhouse. Any pipe system which is thermo-syphoned, however, whether heated by solid fuel or by oil, will be demanding on effort, but these can be made easier to control if fitted, respectively, with a thermostatic flue regulator or a thermostatic control which automatically lights or extinguishes the flame. A pipe system which depends exclusively on a circulating pump can be controlled through a thermostat linked to the pump itself, rather than to the boiler. This means that the boiler can be left to reach its own temperature and is constantly poised to supply heat, but is dangerous if pipes are made of cast iron, for these may be damaged by sudden expansion.

In a porch or conservatory it is tempting to install off-peak storage heaters which run off the domestic supply, but these may not be very efficient. A simple on/off heater will, for example, produce too much heat on a warm day following a cold night. Even with a storage heater which has a controllable input and output you may need to fit proper ventilators to regulate the temperature effectively. Another alternative is to heat your porch or conservatory with narrow hot water pipes from the household supply, but control will again be a problem if your time-switch is set to halt the heater overnight. Better still, keep the boiler temperature constant. Link one time control clock to the circulating pump of the domestic supply and fit a separate pump to the conservatory system. If the conservatory system is self-contained it can be regulated with temperature-sensitive valves within the pipes. Hot air heating will present you with very similar problems, so always take the trouble to seek expert help.

VENTILATION AND SHADING

Controlling the heat of a greenhouse is closely linked with other environmental problems, especially those of ventilation (Fig. 16) and shade. Because warm air is lighter than cold air it rises and if this air escapes through ventilators then heat, and also humidity, can be controlled with ease. The best place for vents is usually – though not inevitably – the highest point of the greenhouse. As the hot air escapes cold air is drawn in through the vents, either by simple exchange or under the pressure of the wind. It comes in, too, through glass overlaps, gaps under the door and any other poor fittings.

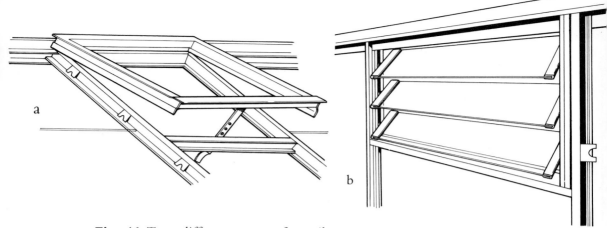

Fig. 16 Two different types of ventilator.
(a) is the fan-light type, and (b) the louvre type.

The rate at which air change takes place depends mainly on the size and position of the ventilators. Ventilators placed low down, through which cool air will rush in, can speed up the air change enormously. Fit ones of louvre design which you can open or close at your own discretion and if possible make sure that the total area of top ventilator is at least one sixth of the floor area, calculated with the vents wide open, though, in fact, many small greenhouses are poorly supplied with ventilation and you may have to settle for less than the perfect situation.

Extractor fans (Fig. 17) are first rate for greenhouse ventilation, with the proviso that they change the air 50–60 times per hour and that they do not create high wind speeds which could damage plants or slow their growth. The best fans, therefore, are large ones, with slow rotations and overlapped so that air will not enter when the fan is not working. Make sure that there is a good air inlet opposite the fan. For even greater control you can fit the fan with a time-switch.

Fan-light roof ventilators and louvre ventilators can be automatically controlled by ventilator arms. These open and close the vents automatically according to temperature (Fig. 18). They are reasonably priced and need no power source as they are powered by natural heat. They can be pre-set to open at a required temperature.

Another way of cutting down heat in the greenhouse is by shading. Roller blinds are effective and can be fixed either inside or outside the greenhouse. Although it gives you less flexibility, painting the outside of the glass with a proprietary liquid shading material is equally effective, as the whiteness reflects, rather than absorbs sunlight. It should be washed off in the autumn so that plants get as much light as possible during the winter months.

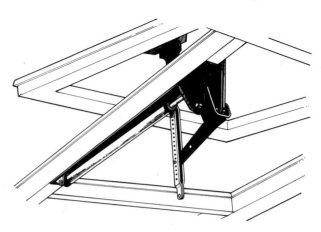

Fig. 17 Extractor fan. This model is fully automatic, switching on only when the temperature rises to a predetermined level.

Fig. 18 Automatic ventilator opener. Expansion type ventilators open and close automatically and are highly efficient.

A range of varieties of greenhouse decorative chrysanthemums will provide flowers from early autumn to mid-winter. This is "yellow Princess Anne".

CHAPTER 2

BASIC EQUIPMENT

BENCHES AND SHELVES

Benches or staging, and shelves, are essential for growing pot plants and for plant propagation. Single-level bench-type staging is often used but tiered staging (two or more levels) makes much better use of the vertical space. The main staging should be set at about waist height with a maximum width of 91 cm (3 ft) so that all plants can be reached easily. Leave a gap between the staging and walls to allow good air circulation and heat to rise. Staging can be fitted along one or both sides of a greenhouse, according to the amount needed.

Staging does not have to be a permanent fixture: many kinds of aluminium staging are easily dismantled and removed to make room for tall summer crops like tomatoes. Modern aluminium staging can often be extended in both length and height later on if the need arises.

It is preferable to erect aluminium staging in an aluminium-framed greenhouse and timber staging in a wooden-framed house.

There are several staging surfaces to choose from. Slatted or openwork surfaces allow surplus water to drain away quickly, ensure good air circulation between plants and allow heat to rise. Staging can be provided with gravel trays to hold gravel, shingle or horticultural aggregate which can be kept moist to create extra humidity around plants — desirable for many kinds of plants in summer.

Shelves, fixed high up, are very useful for keeping plants near the light during the winter months. Or you can have two tiers of staging. Use the upper tier for propagation, seedlings and so on, the lower tier for storing dahlia tubers or chrysanthemum stools over the winter.

WATERING

Your greenhouse wartering equipment need amount to nothing more than a watering can and a cold water tap, but you may want to follow the lead of commercial greenhouse gardeners and install an automatic watering system (Fig. 19). Water is sprayed on to the plants from above or at soil level, or reaches pot plants through individual tubes.

Rather than fitting a completely automatic system, many amateur gardeners prefer to water their greenhouses with a fine mist from a special pipe called a sprayline. These spraylines are easy to fit into a small greenhouse, and will work well as long as the pressure and volume of the water are high enough. Electrically-operated valves can be attached to the system, and these inexpensive devices mean that you can direct water on to your plants at the flick of a switch.

When choosing watering cans for the house select those with long spouts and fine roses, in either metal or plastic.

If you decide to specialize in growing pot plants it might be well worth considering a capillary watering system (Fig. 20), though you can use one for other growing projects too. In principle, a completely level solid bench is lined with polythene to make a completely watertight basin 7.5 or 10 cm (3 or 4 in) deep, and a perforated pipe placed to run down the centre of the bench. The basin is then filled with rough, gritty sand which will draw up the water.

The pipe for the capillary bench is best placed inside some drainage tiles as this will help prevent the holes in the pipe from getting blocked. By attaching the bottom end of the pipe to a fish tank fitted with a ball cock it is easy to keep a steady water level between 12 and 25 mm (½ and 1 in) below the surface of the sand. Or you can operate a capillary set-up with a slow-running hose or possibly special drip nozzles which, as their name suggests, drip water constantly on to the sand. For the greatest possible sophistication, the water input can be electronically controlled.

Placed on top of the sand in the bench, pot plants will absorb water by capillary action – the sucking power is produced by the plant roots

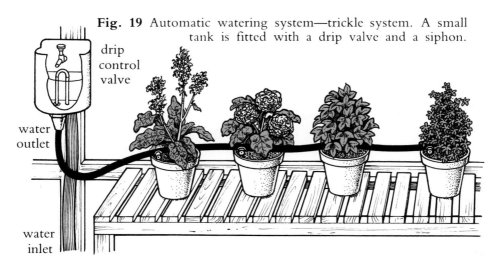

Fig. 19 Automatic watering system—trickle system. A small tank is fitted with a drip valve and a siphon.

drip control valve

water outlet

water inlet

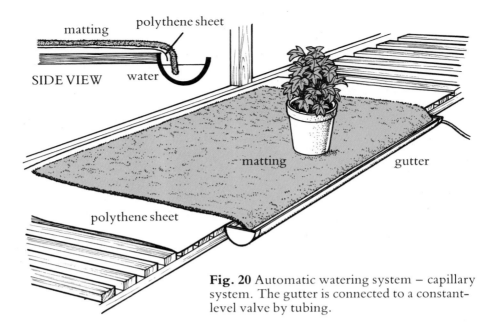

matting
polythene sheet
SIDE VIEW   water

matting   gutter

polythene sheet

Fig. 20 Automatic watering system – capillary system. The gutter is connected to a constant-level valve by tubing.

and by the water-attracting properties of the sand. As long as you do not make them too strong, solutions of mineral nutrients can be added to the bench. Choose plastic rather than clay pots. They will work more efficiently. Once constructed, a capillary bench like this is easy to adapt for growing tomatoes by the 'ring culture' method (see p. 82) and for other crops.

Of course, sand is heavy so a really strong permanent bench will be needed. The alternative is to surface a lighter bench with polythene sheet and capillary watering matting (rather like thick felt), which holds water just as effectively. The matting can be kept moist in several ways, among them by using drip nozzles. Some manufacturers supply complete capillary irrigation systems based on such matting, which are easy to install.

SOIL WARMING

The soil in your greenhouse borders or benches can be adapted to grow heat-loving plants simply by warming it, or you can get good results by warming the benches or pots themselves. Provided the growing medium is warm, many plants will grow well in cool air. This means that the growing medium – soil, bench or pot – can be kept warm very cheaply, and that there is no need to heat the whole greenhouse. The warming process is particularly effective if used *before* planting tomatoes or other plants that thrive on heat. For while the soil quickly heats up if warmed directly, the same process takes a long time, and is

A collection of alpines will provide colour in the unheated greenhouse during winter and spring.

much more costly, if only the air in the greenhouse is warmed by pipes which do not touch the growing medium. Another advantage of soil warming is in the field of propagation. Often you will want to heat a small amount of soil or compost to a high temperature to assist rapid rooting. If so a soil-warming system will prove invaluable.

The soil, or sand on a propagating bench, is warmed by electric soil-warming cables laid in the soil or sand. These are controlled by a thermostat. You can buy complete kits and the system should be set up according to the maker's instructions.

PROPAGATION UNITS

Success in propagation will depend almost entirely on your ability to persuade cuttings of stems or leaves to make roots, and thus become self-supporting, as quickly as possible. The greatest problem is to keep the stem healthy all the while, for viable roots are unlikely to form if soft leaf tissue above ground is in the process of wilting. But in a propagation case the temperature and humidity of the air are higher than normal. The loss of moisture from the leaves – a process called transpiration – is thus cut down to a minimum. The tissues of stem and leaf stay full of water and stiff, making propagation much easier, root formation more rapid.

The most humble sort of propagating case is a polythene bag. Placed over a box or pot it will efficiently retain both heat and moisture. A sheet of glass over a box will have the same effect. More complex propagating cases consist of a solid bench, which can be filled with the

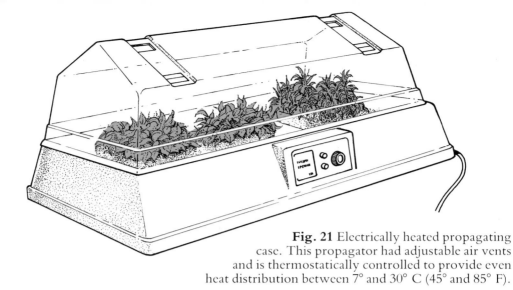

Fig. 21 Electrically heated propagating case. This propagator had adjustable air vents and is thermostatically controlled to provide even heat distribution between 7° and 30° C (45° and 85° F).

growing medium, and which is heated with soil-warming cables, covered by a 'frame' made of glass or polythene. In addition the case can be fully lit and the whole carefully controlled by means of a thermostat, quite independently of the temperature and humidity of the greenhouse itself.

One disadvantage of propagating cases is that they may get too hot and, in turn, damage the plants. To avoid this, you could consider installing a mist propagation unit, which heats the soil to a constant temperature of 21–24° C (70–75° F) while at the same time spraying the cuttings intermittently with a fine mist of water from spray nozzles.

Many electrically heated propagating cases are available, large and small, with or without thermostatic control, from different manufacturers (Fig. 21). There is also a proprietary heated bench which can be used for propagation. The simplest propagators are just heated trays and flexible foil sheets with heating elements sealed in. There is also a small enclosed mist-propagation unit, which is portable.

LIGHTING

Although you may want to light your greenhouse to change the length of the day or intensify the radiance of the sun in spring or autumn, the main use of lighting is to make working in the greenhouse possible in winter and during the evenings. Make sure that you fix the lights in positions which do not cast too much shadow and where you do not have to constantly duck to avoid them. This will throw light out to best advantage all over the greenhouse. And you can add extra bulbs to light benches or dark corners which you use frequently in winter. Do choose waterproof light fittings.

CHAPTER 3

CARING FOR GREENHOUSE PLANTS

Knowing something about the way plants live and grow will help you become an expert in your greenhouse. A good mother appreciates the needs of her baby and, in the same way, a good gardener knows just what will make the plants in his or her care thrive. All green plants have roots, stems and leaves and most bear flowers which mature into fruits containing seeds.

THE GREENHOUSE ENVIRONMENT

Because a greenhouse can overcome the changeability of the weather it will not only support exotic blooms in their natural state but also plants which the breeder has tailored to fruit or flower at times convenient to Man. Although not entirely successful, plant breeding has resulted in a vast range of plants in which the best qualities of different groups and varieties are blended to give the best quality, colour, disease resistance, fruit production and so on.

The really important thing about a greenhouse is that although it supports plants whose growth cycle is essentially similar from seed or cutting to mature plant, these plants are often far from their natural homes and habitats and so need special care. Tropical plants are not, for example, merely tender and sensitive to frost. Tomatoes, whose original home was sunny South America, yearn, despite intense breeding, for all the light they can get, especially in their early days when we try to persuade them to grow in our dreary winters. Plants from the world's tropical forests crave for the hot, humid, shady environment typical of their home. And a lot of perfectly hardy plants find their way into the greenhouse because there they will grow at an unusual season of the year. Lettuce, for example, is supremely successful out-of-doors in summer but will thrive during the winter in a heated or unheated greenhouse.

The artificial conditions of the greenhouse call for thoroughness and patience when growing plants. Inside the house there is light and air but no moisture unless you supply it. The sun shines in summer and there is an excessive build-up of heat which has to be remedied. In winter when there is little or no sunshine you have to produce a substitute. In these warm, often humid conditions plants grow much more quickly and so need more water and more food than those growing outside.

Another important side-effect of the greenhouse's man-made atmosphere is that there is a tremendous difference between the conditions within during day and night. This is especially so in spring and autumn when warm sunny days are often followed by cold nights. The result is a huge temperature variation which can result in unbalanced growth.

One of the great advantages of the greenhouse over the great outside is that whereas out-of-doors the results of your efforts will be, after a few years, quite unpredictable, in the greenhouse you can control and predict plant behaviour with considerable accuracy. To get the most out of your greenhouse take advantage of these special features. Compared with the garden you can start with soil or compost which is free from pests and diseases and whose physical properties are precisely what you want them to be. You start with no weeds, none will arrive unless you introduce them and you can add or subtract heat, light and nutrients at will. Because you have such power use it carefully and do not take chances with doubtful seeds, soil, composts or cuttings. The same factors of total environmental control which enable the plant we grow in the greenhouse to thrive will also enable weeds, pests and diseases to flourish once they get a hold.

The first essentials for plant growth are light, air and water, plus heat, either to trigger growth or to induce a cutting to produce roots. The demand for these front-line supplies increases as the plant grows. How much it rises is governed to a large extent by how large the plant becomes, by the weather and by the time of year. But plants also need minerals which are mostly absorbed from the soil via the roots and transported within the plant to the sites of growth, flower or fruit production. To help the greenhouse gardener balance the mineral needs of the plants in his care fertilizers, liquid feeds and composts are available in vast numbers. But it is as well to know something about what they contain and what the plant will need before you go ahead with any dosage, either to the soil or direct to leaves and stems, for plants can absorb nutrients from these parts as well as from the roots.

PLANT NUTRIENTS

No two plants will thrive on exactly the same diet, nor will a seedling necessarily need the same diet as it will when a mature plant. What is most important is a proper *balance* of nutrients, for just as the human frame needs proteins, carbohydrates, fats and vitamins, but in varying

Left The bougainvillea or paper flower is a popular climber for the intermediate greenhouse. It comes in many brilliant colours.

Right Regal pelargoniums are among the top ten summer flowering pot plants. There are many varieties and colours.

amounts, so plants need a mixture of minerals such as nitrogen, potassium and phosphorus.

Another reason for keeping a constant check on the balance of plant nutrients is that plants grow more quickly in the greenhouse than they do out-of-doors. Their requirements therefore change more rapidly and plant nutrients must be well maintained during the growing period.

The sort of plants which will grow well in any soil depends to a large extent on the acidity or alkalinity of the soil. The substance which has the greatest effect on this important quality is lime. In chemical terms lime is made up of the substance calcium carbonate, which is an alkali. Plants need lime and the calcium carbonate also helps to keep the soil sweet by neutralizing the acids·manufactured by micro-organisms.

Chemists record acidity or alkalinity by a number known as the pH value. A lime-rich soil will have a pH of about 8, an acid-rich soil like peat a pH of around 4. The ideal pH for the greenhouse varies from plant to plant, but many will thrive in pure peat or a mixture of peat and sand. But unlike the peat of natural bogland, greenhouse peat preparations contain few micro-organisms so that little acid is produced and the environment remains stable.

Four chemical elements are essential for the health of all plants:

NITROGEN
Plants absorb nitrogen from the soil in the form of chemical

compounds called nitrates. Nitrogen is needed for the development of the leaves and probably for all plant growth. But any plant will suffer if you give it either too much or too little nitrogen. An excess of nitrogen, particularly an excess in relation to the amount of potassium the plant is getting, will lead to large fleshy leaves and small flowers and fruits. When nitrogen is in short supply the reverse happens. The leaves are small, flowers and fruits of normal size. The colour of the leaves is a good guide to the amount of nitrogen being supplied. Pale green or yellow means too little, a very dark green too much.

POTASSIUM
The role of potassium in the life of plants is a complex one. It is involved in photosynthesis, the process by which, with the help of the green pigment, chlorophyll, in their leaves, plants trap carbon dioxide and combine it with water to make carbohydrates. Potassium is vital to the formation of fruits and seeds and to the manufacture of chlorophyll itself. Give plants potassium in the form of potash – chemically potassium oxide – or as other compounds such as potassium carbonate. The leaves will give you the clues to dosage. Too much potassium results in hard dark leaves, too little in flabby pale-green growth. Experience will give you the best guide but remember that many crops, especially tomatoes, absorb nitrogen and potassium together. Give too much of one and the plant will not be able to take in the other, so take the trouble to balance each one carefully.

PHOSPHORUS
Found in the soil in chemical combinations call phosphates, phosphorus is essential to plants because it is involved in the growth and development of roots, stems, leaves and flowers. Without phosphorus plants cannot use the carbohydrates they build up in photosynthesis and cannot manufacture new cells. Good root production and early maturity are both impossible without phosphorus but an excess or deficiency of this element is very difficult to pinpoint just by looking at a plant. The best guide to a phosphorus shortage, however, is a dark-green or bluish tinge on the leaves.

MAGNESIUM
Like potassium, magnesium is involved in the vital process of photosynthesis. Some crops, including tomatoes, have large demands for magnesium but the element is absorbed alongside potassium and both elements are needed for proper magnesium uptake. Most soils have plenty of natural magnesium but a plant suffering from a lack of it

will have pale leaves which later turn bronze. Too much magnesium is a rare problem and unlikely to cause trouble.

THE BASIC INGREDIENTS OF COMPOSTS

Good feeding in the greenhouse will be enhanced if you put plant roots in high-quality soil or some other growing medium. While ordinary garden soil may be enriched with compost or 'humus' formed from the breakdown of grass cuttings and other garden refuse, professional gardeners usually use the word compost to mean specially-prepared mixtures, enriched with nutrients, which form an excellent environment for the roots of greenhouse plants.

Composts are mixtures of various substances, as follows:

LOAM
Loam is the end-product of the partial rotting of turf from a grass pasture 10–15 cm (4–6 in) thick stacked grass-downwards for about 6 months. Depending on the soil and the quality of the grass loam can vary enormously. Really reliable loam is difficult to come by but a good substitute is the top 22–30 cm (9–12 in) of the soil, though this will be low in organic matter and variable in mineral supply. If using this 'second best' loam always avoid soil which you know has been infested with diseases and pests and choose material whose particles are neither too coarse like sand nor too fine like clay. Check the acidity of the loam and sterilize it.

PEAT
A greenhouse gardener can choose from many different kinds of peat but the ideal peat for composts is light in colour and open in texture: sphagnum moss peat. Avoid dark fine 'dirty' peats or those with a black decomposed look, or use them sparingly with sphagnum peat to step up its mineral content. If in doubt wet the peat and press out the water. The darker it is the less desirable the peat.

In compost good-quality peat acts like a sponge and so helps the growing medium to store both water and vital nutrients. And at the same time it allows air to get to the plant roots. A high-quality peat, supplied in a polythene bag or bale to keep it moist, can be guaranteed to be free of pests and disease-carrying micro-organisms. Peat is most valuable to plants in the long, rather than the short term. The minerals it contains cannot be used immediately but over a matter of months peat encourages growth of micro-organisms which in turn make the nutrients absorbable.

LEAF-MOULD

Once used very widely in compost-making, leaf-mould has fallen from favour because its quality is too variable. Despite this you can make good use of a well-matured leaf-mould from a mixed deciduous wood. Compost containing leaf-mould is particularly good for tomatoes and chrysanthemums which demand nourishment over a long period.

SAND

Whatever its 'grain grading' small amounts of sand will give a compost body and porosity. Always select sand that is neither acid nor alkaline. Make sure it is free from contamination and, for preference, intermediate in texture.

VERMICULITE OR PERLITE

These two substances, made repectively of expanded mica and of volcanic ash, are valuable additions to compost as they can absorb large amounts of water. Although their names may be unfamiliar, neither is a newcomer to the horticultural scene and they can be bought from most garden centres.

THE JOHN INNES COMPOSTS

Extremely useful in the greenhouse, John Innes composts were first compounded, and their ingredients standardised by W.J.C. Lawrence and W.J. Newell of the John Innes Horticultural Institution. Although available ready mixed you can make up your own compost to the basic John Innes formula.

John Innes seed compost is for seed sowing. It is especially useful in winter. Its ingredients are:

> two parts (by bulk) of loam, preferably sterilized by heat
> one part (by bulk) of peat
> one part (by bulk) of coarse sand

To every bushel or 8 gallons (36 litres) of the mixture add 21 g (¾ oz) ground limestone and 42 g (1½ oz) superphosphate.

John Innes potting compost has the following composition:

> seven parts (by bulk) of loam
> three parts (by bulk) of peat
> two parts (by bulk) of coarse sand

To this basic mixture other materials are added in varying amounts and each resulting compost given a number. The No. 1 compost is enriched with 21 g (¾ oz) ground limestone, and 113 g (4 oz) John Innes base fertilizer (which is two parts by weight of hoof and horn meal, two parts superphosphate of lime and one part sulphate of potash) in every bushel. For No. 2 compost add 226 g (8 oz) of base fertilizer and 42 g (1½ oz) ground limestone. For No 3 compost add 340 g (12 oz) of base fertilizer and 63 g (2¼ oz) ground limestone.

Each John Innes compost is suited to a particular job in the greenhouse. Choose potting compost No. 1 for young, newly pricked-off seedlings. As long as the seedlings are housed in large enough pots the compost will contain enough nutrients to feed the plants until they are ready for potting on. Do not transplant these seedlings directly into potting compost No. 2. Instead use John Innes No. 1 but add liquid feed as soon as they start to grow vigorously, particularly if the weather is dull, the temperature low.

The No. 2 compost is ideal for potting on into larger pots. Reserve the No. 3 compost for more mature plants, such as chrysanthemums, which will not be damaged by its high fertilizer content.

THE U/C COMPOSTS

Work carried out at the University of California has given the greenhouse gardener another range of composts. There is a great number of different formulae but all are based on sphagnum moss peat and fine sand. To these, various nutrients are added. You can either buy U/C composts already made up, or you can buy the basic substances plus fertilizers to add as you require, but it is worth remembering that U/C composts have very few mineral reserves and that you will have to administer constant feeds of liquid nutrients from early on. Yet these composts are very useful because they are sterile, that is, free from pests and harmful micro-organisms.
There are several popular U/C mixes:

FOR WINTER AND EARLY SPRING
Use equal parts, by bulk, of moss peat and fine sand and add to each bushel or 8 gallons (36 litres):
    5 g (⅕ oz) nitrate of potash
    5 g (⅕ oz) sulphate of potash
    56 g (2 oz) superphosphates
    170 g (6 oz) magnesium limestone
    56 g (2 oz) ground limestone

FOR SPRING AND SUMMER

Use equal amounts by bulk of peat moss and sand. Add to each bushel of the mixture:

    113 g (4 oz) hoof and horn meal
    7g (¼ oz) ammonium nitrate
    28 g (1 oz) sulphate of potash
    56 g (2 oz) superphosphates
    113 g (4 oz) ground limestone
    56 g (2 oz) magnesium limestone

One word of warning. *Never* add the hoof and horn meal until just before you use the compost. Care should be taken not to overwater the U/C composts.

Experience will tell you which recipes work best, but some gardeners prefer to add between 141 and 226 g (5 and 8 oz) of ground limestone to the spring and summer compost, plus a slow-acting fertilizer containing traces of the minerals iron and manganese. Others prefer a mix of 75 per cent peat and 25 per cent sand, yet others the exact reverse of this. A coarse sand may give better results and is certainly more popular than a fine one.

FOR FULL SEASON GROWING

U/C composts can be used in containers but the plants will suffer unless they are constantly fed.

COMPOST MIXING

Always keep your compost ingredients under cover and make sure that they are reasonably dry. The best place for mixing is a concrete floor. First put down the most bulky ingredient (usually loam) followed by peat and sand. Turn the total several times before finally adding the fertilizers, carefully measured. Add each one individually and mix well each time. *Before you use the compost leave it to warm up in the greenhouse.*

CHAPTER 4

POT PLANTS

Though still far from rivalling the Dutch in the number and excellence of their pot plants, Britain's greenhouse gardeners are fast realizing the pleasures of cultivating these members of the indoor team. With a little persistence plus plenty of common sense you can produce a whole galaxy of colour and variety. Your greenhouse will not only provide you with the absorbing interest of pot plants but will ensure plants in your home all the year round.

POT PLANT NEEDS

Pot plants vary enormously in their habits and grow and flower at different times throughout the year. The secret of success is knowing when the plants need water and nutrients, controlling the environment carefully, selecting the right compost and putting it in a pot which is neither too big nor too small. Except for cacti and slow-growing plants like ferns most actively-growing pot plants will need a liquid feed every 10–14 days. Although you may be far from 100 per cent successful, especially at the start, do persevere with pot plants in the greenhouse. With experience you will find them a most rewarding hobby.

As far as equipment is concerned what you need for growing pot plants is a well-situated properly-ventilated greenhouse free from drips. It should have a good clean water supply and a heating system which can maintain a minimum temperature of between 7 and 10° C (45 and 50° F). Inside the greenhouse you will need a fairly extensive layout of benches. A tiered set-up will not only create more space but will make your display look more attractive. Keep a convenient corner of a bench, either in the greenhouse or in a nearby shed, for potting up plants. You may also get good use from a storage area to house compost ingredients, though this is far from essential now that reliably formulated mixtures can be easily obtained. Make sure you have enough room for storing pots and seedboxes and bear in mind the possibility of fixing a permanent propagating case, though you can easily make do with a temporary 'rooting bench' for a few years.

The way you start off your pot plants will depend on the individual

Left Foliage plants make a good foil for spring-flowering cinerarias. These are annual pot plants raised from seed.

Lower left Calceolarias are raised annually from seeds and flower in the spring and summer. They make a long and brilliant show.

Right The autumn and winter flowering cyclamens are not the easiest subjects to grow and need to be kept cool.

Lower right Fuchsias are easy to raise and grow. There are many different varieties and they bloom throughout the summer.

species. Some are started from seeds while others are best propagated from cuttings, which you may have to beg from friends or neighbours, either as cuttings themselves or in the form of stock plants.

FLOWERING PLANTS

The range of pot plants which will thrive in a frost-free greenhouse is enormous but keep to a few simple sorts to begin with. Primulas, pelargoniums, coleus, fuchsias and many annuals make excellent pot plants and are relatively simple to grow. Many cacti are simplicity itself, but tuberous begonias, cinerarias or streptocarpus can be a little more difficult.

ANNUALS IN POTS

Some of the best annuals to grow in pots in the greenhouse to give both colour and cut flowers are:

Acroclinium	Felicia	Nemesia
Antirrhinum	Godetia	Petunia
Arctotis	Larkspur	Ursinia
Calendula	Nasturtium	Zinnia

Sow the seeds in early or mid-spring and pot the seedlings in 7.5 cm (3 in) pots. Then simply supply them with moderate heat. Pot on the young plants to 12.5 cm (5 in) pots.

ORCHIDS

At present there is much interest in orchid-growing but it need not be the exclusive province of the professional. Many orchids merely need a frost-free greenhouse but all demand humidity and shade in summer. The basic compost for orchid-growing is equal parts of sphagnum peat and shredded bark (orchid bark). Add some broken crocks to the pots to give good drainage. Rather than risking disappointment it is well worth taking the time to consult a book devoted to orchid-growing and you can also join one of the orchid societies.

None of the following orchids is difficult.

For the Cool Greenhouse

Coelogyne	Odontoglossum
Cymbidium (especially	Oncidium
miniature varieties)	Paphiopedilum (some)
Dendrobium	

For the Intermediate Greenhouse

Cattleya   × Laeliocattleya
× Brassolaeliocattleya   Paphiopedilum

For the Warm House

Phalaenopsis   Vanda

ALPINES

A cold greenhouse is an excellent place to grow alpine plants. These natives of the world's mountain ranges will make your greenhouse both colourful and interesting. Like orchid-growing this is rather specialized and you will gain much from becoming a member of the Alpine Garden Society. Choice of plants:

Andromeda, *Campanula garganica*, Cassiope, Crocus (winter flowering), Cyclamen, Cytisus, Dianthus, Dodecatheon, Draba, *Dryas octopetala*, Dwarf conifers, Hepatica, Helleborus, Lewisia, Dwarf narcissus, Primula, Rhodohypoxis, Saxifraga, Sedum, Sempervivum.

Many shrubs and herbaceous plants will bloom much earlier if potted and cultivated in the greenhouse. The list of plants is virtually endless.

WALL PLANTS AND SHRUBS

Many tender wall plants and shrubs are ideal occupants for a lean-to greenhouse. Choose, for a start, from any of these:

Cobaea scandens   Bougainvillea   *Plumbago capensis*
Ipomoea rubro-caerulea   *Jasminum polyanthum*

FERNS

You can grow any number of ferns in a greenhouse. They do particularly well on a north-facing side, which is shady and moist. Some ferns which should thrive are:

Adiantum cuneatum   *Pteris cretica* 'Albolineata'
Adiantum decorum   *Pteris cretica* 'Major'
Adiantum elegans   *Pteris tremula*
Cyrtomium falcatum (Holly fern)   *Pteris wimsetti*

Ferns can be propagated in several ways. Many can be successfully grown from spores, but the fern *Asplenium bulbiferum* can be multiplied from small bulb-like structures called bulbils. Other ferns throw out runners from which new plants can be cultivated. A fern easily propagated in this way is *Nephrolepis* : merely peg the minature plants down into the soil where they will root.

Greenhouse Pot Plants (Flowering Plants)

Genus	Species etc.	Ease of Culture	Propagation	Flowering Time	Average Height	Temp. Req.	Notes
ACHIMENES	(various colours)	T	Rhizomes (tubers) early–mid spring	Late spring – early autumn	15–22 cm	I	Dry out rhizomes over winter
APHELANDRA	squarrosa 'Louisae'	T	Cuttings, various times. Use propagation case	Various	30–40 cm	W	Can be difficult to grow and dislikes damp or draughts
AZALEA	Indica	T	Cuttings in spring in propagation case	Xmas on	30–40 cm (12–16 in)	C/I	Grafted plants can be retained for years
BEGONIA	semperflorens	E	Seed late winter/onwards	Early summer – early autumn	15–30 cm (6–12 in)	I	
	tuberous (double)	E	Start tubers late winter	early summer – early autumn	30–38 cm (12–15 in)	I	Tubers rest in winter
	'Gloire de Lorraine'	E	Cuttings late summer	Late autumn	22–30 cm (9–12 in)	I	
			Cuttings late winter/onwards	Late winter			
BELOPERONE	guttata (Shrimp Plant)	E	Cuttings in mid-spring in propagating case	Summer	30–40 cm (12–16 in)	I	Likes a little shade in summer. Give plenty of water
CACTI	various types	E/T	Various methods. Sections of stems etc., also seed	Various	Various	C/I	Dozens of different types. Most can be grown in frost-free greenhouse in J.I. + grit. Give plenty of sun
CALCEOLARIA	herbeohybrida (hybrida multiflora) multiflora nana	T	Seed in mid to late summer	Early to late summer	30–40 cm (12–16 in)	C	Cool steady growth. Put in 12.5–15 cm (5–6 in) pots for flowering
CAMELLIA	japonica	D	Leaf bud cuttings early spring	Winter/early spring	45–60 cm (18–24 in)	C	Lime-free compost essential. Stand in cold frame in summer
CAMPANULA	isophylla	E	Cuttings in early spring	Summer	Pendulous	C	Ideal for hanging baskets or edge of staging
CAPSICUM (grown for decorative fruit)	annuum	E	Seed in late winter	Autumn on	25–30 cm (10–12 in)	C	Keep cool. Shade if necessary. Spray frequently when flowering to assist fruit formation
CELOSIA	plumosa	E	Seed in late winter	Late spring – early autumn	38 cm (15 in)	C	A fairly simple plant to grow. Gives good colour and lots of interest

Key   D = Difficult; E = Easy; T = Tricky.

C = Cool; I = Intermediate; W = Warm

CHRYSANTHEMUMS (in pots)—See Chapter 7

CINERARIA	grandiflora, multiflora, multiflora nana	T	Seed late spring/early summer	Spring on	30–38 cm (12–15 in)	C	Place outside in summer in shaded position. Keep cool in greenhouse. Best on slatted open bench
CRASSULA	(Rochea) coccinea	E	Cuttings in spring	Early summer on	22–25 cm (9–10 in)	C	Add lime to compost. Cold frames in summer
CYCLAMEN	persicum	D	Seed space sown (120 seeds per tray) early autumn–mid-winter. Pot early and keep tuber above soil level. Tubers can be potted in late summer	Late summer on	22–25 cm (9–10 in)	C	Flowers in 12.5–15 cm (5–6 in) pot. Cold frame or cool greenhouse in summer. Regular feeding essential
ECHEVERIA	retusa	E	Sections of stem with rosette of leaves after flowering	Winter	22–25 cm (9–10 in)	C/I	A relatively easy plant to grow, but dislikes overwatering
ERICA (Heath)	gracilis, gracilis alba, nivalis, hyemalis	T	Tip of stem cuttings in late autumn/mid-winter. Root in 3 parts peat, 1 part sand in propagating case	Throughout winter	30–45 cm (12–18 in)	C	Lime-free compost (J.I.+flowers of sulphur, without lime). Stop frequently to encourage bushy growth. Takes 2 years to develop.
FUCHSIA	(many different varieties)	E	Internodal cuttings spring, individual containers. Root in propagating case	Summer/autumn	Various	C	Frequent feeding essential. Give plenty of air and water in later stages of growth.
GENISTA	(Cytisus canariensis)	E	Cuttings mid-winter/mid-spring. Takes 2 years to produce good plant	Spring	30–60 cm (12–24 in)	C	Really a shrub. Merely requires cool growing and regular trimming to keep bushy. Stand outside and keep shaded during second season. Lift in for winter

Genus	Species etc.	Ease of Culture	Propagation	Flowering Time	Average Height	Temp. Req.	Notes
GERANIUM	(Zonal Pelargonium) (Regal Pelargonium) Many lovely varieties. Ivy-leaved, especially for hanging baskets. Scented, variegated	E	Cuttings at various times of year. Autumn or spring. Individual containers or open propagating bench	Long flowering period	Various	C	One of the easiest plants to grow. Do not overwater and keep feeding
GLOXINIA		T	Seed in mid- to late winter. Tubers, spring in propagating case	Late summer/early autumn	22–30 cm (9–12 in)	I	Needs constant watering and feeding
HIPPEASTRUM	(Amaryllis)	T	Pot bulb in 12.5–15 cm (5–6 in) pot for starting in spring, early winter or sooner	Mid-winter/spring	45–50 cm (18–20 in)	I	
HYDRANGEA	macrophylla (Many excellent varieties)	D	Internodal stem cuttings late winter/late spring (non-flowering shoots only). Trim leaves to reduce transpiration loss	Spring	40–45 cm (116–20 in) or taller	C/I	Stand outside in summer, or in cold frame. Pinch plant to encourage leaf growth. Keep nitrogen and phosphate levels low during feeding. Use iron sequestrene if foliage turns white. Apply blueing compound to intensify blue colour
IMPATIENS	wallerana (Busy Lizzie)	E	Seed late winter/ early spring or cuttings at various times	Summer	25–38 cm (10–15 in)	C/I	A very simple plant to grow. Must have plenty of light
MARGUERITE	(Chrysanthemum frutescens) (white) (C. coronarium) (yellow)	E	Cuttings late summer – mid-winter Seed late winter	Summer	30–40 cm (12–16 in)	C	Keep cool. Stop frequently to induce bushy plant
POINSETTIA	(Euphorbia pulcherrima)	D	Stem cuttings in late spring	Autumn/ winter	60–120 cm (2–4 ft)	I/W	Stand in frame late summer/early autumn and avoid dryness. Grown for coloured bracts
POLYANTHUS		E	Seed in late spring. Pot into 9 cm (3½ in) pots.	Early spring on	22–30 cm (9–12 in)	C	Stand in frame during summer. Keep cool and well watered. Lift into greenhouse early winter onwards

Genus	Species/variety		Propagation	Flowering	Height	Temp	Notes
PRIMULA	obconica, malacoides, kewensis, sinensis	E	Seed sown thickly late spring–early summer. Pot into 5 in pot	Spring/summer	22–30 cm (9–12 in)	C	Keep slightly moist in winter till flowering starts. Apply iron sequestrene if yellowing of foliage occurs. Note: Many people are allergic to Primulas, (cause a rash)
ROSES	dwarf types	T	Buy in and pot in 12.5 cm (5 in) pots early to mid-winter and cut hard back	Summer	40–45 cm (16–18 in)	C/I	The object is merely to advance flowering. Use a good compost and keep feeding
SAINTPAULIA	ionantha	T	Seed in spring (do not come true from seed). Leaf stalk cuttings. Shade from direct light	Flower over a long period	15–22 cm (6–9 in)	I/W	Feed regularly with high potash feed. Keep well watered and warm. Avoid draughts
SALPIGLOSSIS	CT	Seed in early autumn	Late spring	60–90 cm (2–3 ft)	C	Grow cool	
SALVIA	splendens	E	Seed in mid to late winter. Flowers in 12.5 cm (5 in) pot	Summer	22–30 cm (9–12 in)	C	Really a bedding plant, but excellent in pots. Keep cool in summer
SCHIZANTHUS	(Poor Man's Orchid)	E	Seed late summer	Mid to late spring	30–60 cm (12–24 in)	C	Grow cool. Give plenty of light and adequate support. Pinch out to ensure bushy growth
SCHLUMBERGERA	× buckleyi (Xmas Cactus)	E	Sections of stem segments in spring	Mid-winter on	pendulous	C	Keep cool in summer. Give plenty of water. Repot occasionally
SOLANUM	capsicastrum, pseudocapsicum (attractive berries)	T	Seed in late winter. Sow 150 per tray. Cuttings in late winter in propagating case	Winter, especially mid-winter	30–40 cm (12–16 in)	I	Stand in shady frames in summer, lifting out during early autumn. Always add Epsom salts, 21 g (¾ oz) per bushel. Stop plant height to induce bushy growth. Syringe frequently during flowering to induce setting.
STOCKS	Beauty of Nice	E	Seed mid to late summer	Spring	45 cm (18 in)	C	Keep cool and airy
STREPTOCARPUS		T	Seed mid-winter to early spring. Leaf-cuttings in late summer	Late summer/mid autumn	22 cm (9 in)	C	Feed and water regularly
ZANTEDESCHIA	aethiopica (Arum)	E	Division in mid to late summer	Mid-spring on	60–90 cm (2–3 ft)	C/I	Rest outdoors in summer before repotting

Greenhouse Pot Plants (Foliage Plants)

Genus	Species etc.	Propagation	Height	Temp.	Notes
BEGONIA	rex (Many other types)	Leaf or stem cuttings anytime in propagating case	30–60 cm (12–24 in) and taller	I/W	Water sparingly in winter
CHLOROPHYTUM	comosum 'Variegatum' (Spider Plant)	Layer small plantlets to ground	30–45 cm (12–18 in)	C	Easy plant to grow
CISSUS	antarctica (Kangaroo Vine)	Leaf bud or terminal cuttings	Climber	I	An excellent foliage plant. Keep well supported
COLEUS	blumei (Many colour forms)	Seed – variable colours. Cuttings rooted in propagating case in spring	30–60 cm (1–2 ft)	C/I	Must have plenty of light. Keep well watered
CROTON	Codiaeum variegatum	Cuttings with at least 6–7 leaves. Also leaf bud cuttings. Both in propagating case	30–60 cm (1–2 ft)	W	Give full light, shade only in full sun
DIEFFENBACHIA	picta (Dumb Cane)	Terminal and stem cuttings, the latter with 2 buds horizontally. Both in propagating case	30–60 cm (1–2 ft)	I/W	A fairly easy plant to grow
DRACAENA	(inc. Cordyline)	Stem cuttings. Cordyline australis and C. terminalis from seed late winter/early spring	45 cm (18 in)	I/W	Shade and high humidity necessary
FATSHEDERA	(a cross between Fatsia japonica and Hedera helix)	Terminal and leaf bud cuttings in propagating case	45–60 cm (18–24 in)	C	Must be well supported
FATSIA	japonica	Root cuttings in early spring	60–90 cm (2–3 ft)	C	Green fig-like leaves
FICUS	elastica 'Decora', lyrata (Fiddle-leaf Fig) pumila	Leaf bud and terminal cuttings in propagating case	30–180 cm (1–6 ft)	I/W	Not the easiest plants to grow
GREVILLEA	robusta (Silk Oak)	Seed late autumn/early spring	60 cm (2 ft)	C	Cool and shade required
HEDERA	(the ivies)	Tips or leaf cuttings any time	Trailing	C	Easy to grow. Ideal for edge of staging
HYPOESTES	phyllostachya	Seeds, spring	30 cm (12 in)	I	Easy to grow
MARANTA	leuconeura 'Kerchoveana'	Division of roots in spring	30–60 cm (1–2 ft)	I/W	Easily grown
PEPERÒMIA	argyreia (obtusifolia)	Leaf cuttings in propagating case	22–30 cm (9–12 in)	I/W	Easy to cultivate

PHILODENDRON	(Various species and number of related plants such as Scindapsus aureus and Monstera deliciosa)	Leaf bud cutting in propagating case	30–90 cm (12–36 in)	I/W	Needs support, shade from sun
PILEA	cadierei	Nodal or terminal cuttings in propagating case	22–30 cm (9–12 in)	I	An easy plant to grow
RHOICISSUS	rhomboidea (Grape Ivy)	Leaf bud or heeled cuttings in propagating case	1.8 m (6 ft)	I	Needs support
RICINUS	communis (Castor Oil Plant) plus varieties	Seed in late winter/early spring	90–120 cm (3–4 ft)	I	Give plenty of light
SANSEVIERIA	trifasciata (Mother-in-Law's Tongue or Bowstring Hemp)	Cuttings from leaf tip or suckers (variegated types)	40–45 cm (16–18 in)	I	An indestructible plant. Easy to grow
SAXIFRAGA	stolonifera (Mother-of-Thousands)	Runners, division or from seed	7.5 cm (3 in)	C	One of the easiest plants to grow
SELAGINELLA	(Many different types)	Cuttings	10–15 cm (4–6 in)	I	A useful plant for greenhouse staging
TRADESCANTIA	(Various kinds including Zebrina-Wandering Jew)	Cuttings	Trailing	I	Easily grown plant with variegated leaves. Ideal for edge of greenhouse staging

Spring-flowering *Primula obconica* is an easy pot plant and should be kept cool and moist.

CHAPTER 5

BULB FORCING

Although it need not be done in a greenhouse, bulb forcing is a hobby which offers any gardener plenty of scope for producing showy flowers in large numbers and well before outdoor bulbs have burst into bloom. Bulbs are easy to deal with, and need little or no artificial heat, but do select renowned, reliable suppliers. High-class bulbs cost little more than poor-quality specimens, yet the extra money is a good insurance against disappointment.

CHOOSING AND PLANTING BULBS

The bulbs which will flower the earliest are usually specially treated by the growers and can be bought ready planted in bowls full of fibre or can be planted in bulb fibre in boxes or pots in your own greenhouse, with the tip of the bulb just showing. Plant in early autumn.

Because rooting is quickest and most prolific at low temperatures, put the planted bulbs in a cold frame, a sheltered corner of the garden or in a cellar and cover them with moist peat or old ashes. They are unlikely to need watering but if the weather is very dry, give the fibre an occasional but thorough hosing.

Once the shoots are green and have pushed well above ground, so that 3.8–5 cm (1½–2 in) are showing, lift the bulbs into an intermediate or cool greenhouse. At first keep tulips and hyacinths in subdued light, daffodils in full light. After 7–10 days, when the flower stems are well lengthened, give them more heat and full light either in the greenhouse or in your house. Later flowering bulbs can, however, be brought straight into the light, but whichever method you choose always make sure the bulbs do not dry out.

Many bulbs, but particularly tulips and daffodils do well if planted in greenhouse borders. There they will give you cut flowers early on in the year. For pot-planted bulbs, an alternative to bringing them out from darkness to daylight is to force them to flower in artificial light at a temperature of 18–21° C (65–70° F). A warm cellar or cupboard is ideal for the purpose. For every m² (square yard) of space you will need one 100 watt bulb. Switch these lights on for 12 hours in every 24. The greatest disadvantage of forcing bulbs in artificial light is that they tend, especially daffodils, to sprout too many leaves and not enough flowers.

DAFFODILS

One of the largest and least troublesome of groups, the daffodils or narcissi offer a greenhouse gardener an enormous choice. For the earliest flowers choose well-established varieties like 'Paper White' and 'Grand Soleil d'Or'. For later on yellow trumpet daffodils, like 'Golden Harvest', are highly recommended.

Pot daffodils in proprietary bulb fibre. Keep them covered with peat or ashes, in the dark, until the spears of the leaves look green and you can feel the flower bud clear of the neck of the bulb, then give them constant light and air. By late autumn the early flowerers will need some warmth, while the rest will appreciate a rise in temperature from early winter through to early spring. Avoid high temperatures until the bud is fully out of the bulb. Always stake daffodils well to stop them bending and breaking.

TULIPS

In myriad varieties, growing in number year by year, will flower in pots from early winter until the end of spring. Popular tulips for forcing include 'Brilliant Star', 'Christmas Marvel', 'Marshal Joffre', 'Princess Margaret' and 'Scarlet Cardinal'. Pot in early or mid-autumn in bulb fibre. Force your tulips by first plunging them into peat. As soon as shoots appear they can have constant light.

CROCUSES

Most crocuses flower early and if planted in good time – early autumn – will bloom in mid- or late winter, or even early winter. After planting cover the pots with peat or ashes for five weeks then keep them in a cold frame until early or mid-winter when you can bring them into warmth. Try to avoid sharp temperature changes, especially from cold to hot. They will make the foliage grow long and spindly and the blooms may fail.

GLADIOLI

These beautiful corms will flower much earlier in the greenhouse than out-of-doors but you cannot force them as hard as tulips or daffodils. For the best results put them in greenhouse borders filled with a rich loam 15 cm (6 in) apart and 7.5 cm (3 in) below the soil surface in late winter or early spring. Or put the largest ones in 20–22 cm (8–9 in) pots. Choose early-flowering varieties.

BULBS FOR FORCING

DAFFODILS

For Christmas 'Paper White', 'Grand Soleil d'Or'.

Mid-winter onwards 'Golden Harvest', 'King Alfred', 'Mrs. R. O. Backhouse', 'February Gold', 'Cheerfulness', 'Silver Chimes', 'Polar Ice'.

HYACINTHS

Blue 'King of the Blues' (deep blue), 'Ostara' (deep blue, very early), 'Bismark' (pale blue).

Pink and Red 'Lady Derby' (pale pink), 'Jan Bos' (bright red), 'Pink Pearl' (deep pink), 'Salmonetta' (apricot salmon).

White 'Carnegie' (pure white), 'L'Innocence' (pure white, large bells).

Yellow 'City of Haarlem' (clear yellow), 'Yellow Hammer' (golden yellow, early).

TULIPS

Early 'Brilliant Star' (scarlet), 'Marshal Joffre' (yellow).

Early Double 'Peach Blossom' (deep pink), 'Electra' (cherry red), 'Mr Van der Hoef' (rich yellow).

HYACINTHS
With a little forethought you should be able to have these heady-scented flowers in bloom for Christmas. Pot Roman hyacinths in late summer or early autumn and keep them under peat for about 5 weeks. By late autumn you should be able to bring them into a slightly-warmed greenhouse in full light. Following Roman hyacinths, plant other varieties to give a good show right through until mid-spring.

IRISES
Like gladioli, irises can be planted in the spring but there are many varieties which will give you colour in early and mid-spring if planted in the autumn. Do not force these irises but plant them in borders or pots in the greenhouse and leave them to develop naturally in its sheltered environment. Set them about 7.5 cm (3 in) deep and 7.5–10 cm (3–4 in) apart. Dutch iris are good for autumn planting.

Schizanthus, or poor man's orchid, needs very cool conditions. It is easily raised from seed sown in summer.

FREESIAS

Many people count freesias as their favourite flowers – their scent is delicious, their blooms are bright but delicate. Thanks to modern plant breeding freesias come in a wonderful range of colours. You can either grow freesias from seed or from corms. Sow seed in mid-spring, plant corms in late summer or early autumn.

Freesia corms thrive in a loamy soil and need plenty of ventilation. Until growth starts, cover the pots with 2.5 cm (1 in) of peat, but remove it as soon as the leaves start to show so that they can grow unhindered. At this stage, they can be taken into the greenhouse, but do not let them get too hot – a place near the glass is ideal.

There are three main methods of growing freesias from seed. Firstly, the seeds can be sown in boxes of moist peat, covered with a sheet of glass and paper and kept at a temperature of 13–15° C (55–60° F). Once the germination process is complete, the seedlings can be pricked off 5 cm (2 in) apart into 20 cm (8 in) clay or bituminized pots made of tough paper, filled with John Innes No. 2 or U/C summer mix compost. Secondly, the seeds can be sown direct in the containers, but germination does then tend to be erratic. Thirdly, you can sow the seeds individually into peat blocks, which can then be planted in pots or in greenhouse borders, but this method takes up a lot of greenhouse space and the foliage is far more prolific than the flowers.

During the summer, take the young plants, in boxes or pots, out into a cold frame. Fed and watered regularly, they should make good growth. In early autumn take the plants back to the greenhouse. With water and moderate warmth they will soon flower and will give you many weeks of colour. Help prevent the plants flopping and breaking by supporting them with twiggy sticks.

CHAPTER 6

RAISING SUMMER BEDDING PLANTS

Although many gardeners take the lazy way out and buy summer bedding plants from their local nurseries, there is much more satisfaction in growing your own plants, either from cuttings or from seed. And as well as a sense of achievement you will be able to grow just the colours and varieties you want. The greenhouse is exactly the right place to give these plants a good start in life.

PLANTS IN THE GREENHOUSE

Summer bedding plants which need special care are dahlias and tuberous begonias, as neither will tolerate the slightest frost. Start into growth by bedding the tubers in moist peat during late winter and early spring and giving plenty of warmth. Conventional cuttings of dahlias can then be taken and rooted normally. Or you can store the dahlia tubers in a frost-free place over the winter and plant them out or pot them in mid- to late spring when they should grow naturally.

The easiest and most common way of raising bedding plants is from seed. You will have to sow seeds at different times as some take longer to develop than others. For good measure sow one seed pan of each species you select. As they grow prick the seedlings off into seed trays, or containers with many separate compartments. Watch out for damping off – a fungal disease of seedlings. Once it starts it will spread through a whole batch of seedlings very rapidly and there is little you can do to stop it. This is particularly common in lobelia and antirrhinum, but it is made worse by loam which has been sterilized at high temperatures, for this soil gives off ammonia which, in turn, encourages the growth of the fungus. For this reason choose a soil-free growing medium such as a peat-based seed compost.

The whole spectrum of bedding plants contains, as you might expect, some perennials and some annuals, all half-hardy or tender. For convenience all can be given the same kind of treatment. Your aim should be to have them ready to set out in the garden as soon as the spring displays are over, probably in late spring, though the exact time will vary from district to district and possibly from year to year. In northern areas, or if plants are very tender, be patient and wait until early summer before you expose your carefully-tended greenhouse plants to the rigours of the weather.

PROPAGATION

Although you will want to synchronize your timing, different bedding plants will need different treatments. Seeds are easy and should present you with few problems, but taking cuttings can be more tricky. These cuttings can be taken from half-hardy or tender perennials in early to mid-autumn or taken from the same plants before they are lifted out of their summer beds. As a third alternative, you can take cuttings in the spring from plants which have been overwintered in a frost-free greenhouse.

Clip off sturdy cuttings 7.5 or 10 cm (3 or 4 in) long and, preferably, though not necessarily, without flowers. Trim them and place them 5 cm (2 in) apart in boxes containing a rooting medium of sand, peat and a little clean soil. A frost-free greenhouse will now come into its own, for although the cuttings may survive, root and grow in a sheltered cold frame covered with hessian on frosty nights, the greenhouse will prevent massive loss of cuttings as the result of frost, snow and damp.

Do not struggle or be impatient for quick growth. Large plants produced too soon will be a nuisance rather than an asset. In the same way you can take your time with cuttings from plants which have been overwintered in the greenhouse. But in this case you can encourage the cuttings to root more quickly by keeping them in a warm place, either in boxes or on a warm propagating bench. Pot off the rooted cuttings in 9 cm (3½ in) pots, using John Innes potting compost or U/C summer mix. Grow them on in the greenhouse, then several weeks before planting them out in the garden harden them off in a cold frame. In fact, all bedding plants should be well hardened before they are planted out.

Name	Propagation	Colour	Height	Dist. apart
AGERATUM	Seed in late winter/early spring	Blue	10–22 cm (4–9 in)	15 cm (6 in)
ALYSSUM	Seed in late winter/early spring	White, pink	10–15 cm (4–6 in)	15 cm (6 in)
ANTIRRHINUM	Seed in late winter/early spring	Various	30–45 cm (12–18 in)	25–30 cm (10–12 in)
ASTER	Seed in early spring	Various	30–45 cm (12–18 in)	25–30 cm (10–12 in)
BEGONIA (Fibrous-rooted)	Seed in late winter/early spring	Pink, red, white	22–30 cm (9–12 in)	22–30 cm (9–12 in)
BEGONIA Tuberous	Plant tubers in spring	Various	22–30 cm (9–12 in)	22–30 cm (9–12 in)
CALCEOLARIA	Cuttings autumn/spring	Yellow, red	30–38 cm (12–15 in)	22 cm (9 in)
CARNATION	Seed in spring	Various	30–35 cm (12–14 in)	30 cm (12 in)
DAHLIA	Seed in spring for dwarf bedding types, or cuttings from overwintered tubers when growth starts. Tubers may also be planted	Various	30–180 cm (12–72 in)	30–90 cm (12–36 in) (bedding types at 30 cm (12 in) apart)
DIANTHUS (Pinks)	Seed in late winter	Various	30–38 cm (12–15 in)	25–30 cm (10–12 in)
FUCHSIA	Cuttings taken in spring	Red, pink, purple, etc	45–90 cm (18–36 in)	45–90 cm (18–36 in)
GERANIUM (Zonal pelargonium)	Cuttings spring or autumn; seed in winter	Red, pink, orange, white	22–30 cm (9–12 in)	22–30 cm (9–12 in)
GLADIOLUS	By corms planted direct or started in heat before planting outside in late spring	Vast range of colours	45–90 cm (18–36 in) or more	15–30 cm (6–12 in)
HELIOTROPE	By cuttings or seed in spring	Blue	22–90 cm (9–36 in)	30–90 cm (12–36 in)
IMPATIENS	Seed sown in mid-spring	Various	15–22 cm (6–9 in)	15–22 cm (6–9 in)

Name	Propagation	Colour	Height	Dist. apart
LOBELIA	Seed sown in late winter	Blue, white, pink, red	15–22 cm (6–9 in)	15–22 cm (6–9 in)
MARIGOLD (French and African)	Seed sown in early spring	Orange, yellow, red shades	22–76 cm (9–30 in)	30–38 cm (12–15 in)
MESEMBRYAN-THEMUM	Seed sown in spring	Various.	Carpeting	22–30 cm (9–12 in)
MIMULUS	Seed sown in early spring	Yellows and reds	30–38 cm (12–15 in)	22–30 cm (9–12 in)
NEMESIA	Seed in late winter/early spring	Various	22–30 cm (9–12 in)	30 cm (12 in)
NICOTIANA	Seed in late winter/early spring	Shades of pink, red, white, etc.	30–60 cm (12–24 in)	30 cm (12 in)
PENSTEMON	By cuttings taken in spring or autumn	Various	30–60 cm (12–24 in)	30 cm (12 in)
PETUNIA	Seed in late winter/early spring	Various	30–38 cm (12–15 in)	30 cm (12 in)
PHLOX (drummondii)	Seed in spring	Various	30–38 cm (12–15 in)	25–30 cm (10–12 in)
SALVIA (Scarlet)	By seed in late winter	Scarlet	30 cm (12 in)	22 cm (9 in)
TAGETES	Seed in early spring	Orange, yellow	25–30 cm (10–12 in)	22–30 cm (9–12 in)
VERBENA	Seed in mid to late winter	Various	Trailing	30 cm (12 in)

CHAPTER 7

CHRYSANTHEMUMS

For producing flowers in autumn and early winter chrysanthemums are absolutely unbeatable and deserve a place in every greenhouse. Even the most inexperienced of greenhouse gardeners will get enormous fun from growing chrysanthemums and his living-rooms can be full of colour right through until mid-winter.

THE NEEDS OF CHRYSANTHEMUMS

Although chrysanthemums can be grown out-of-doors the greenhouse is essential if you want blooms after the winter frosts have set in. Most chrysanthemums are grown from cuttings and while these will survive in a cold frame the greenhouse does offer a much more risk-free environment.

Chrysanthemums are interesting plants because, except for some early varieties, they will only form flower buds when the days are short. So unless there are less than 14½ hours of daylight in every 24 you will get no buds or blooms. Botanically chrysanthemums are perennials and the part lodged below ground, the rootstock, is extremely hardy. Flowers and foliage, too, can stand fairly low temperatures but much depends on type and variety. Though outdoors chrysanthemums can only be grown in the months between spring and autumn, in a greenhouse they will flourish all the year round, but without shading they will naturally only flower in the weeks when the days are short.

CHRYSANTHEMUM TYPES

Because there are so many chrysanthemum varieties, and because new ones are constantly appearing, it is difficult to be specific about the best sorts to grow. Rather, find a good catalogue from a specialist chrysanthemum grower and make your own choice of sizes and colours. Visit flower shows, local and national, to get an idea of what is going on or join a chrysanthemum society to hear the latest about varieties and growing methods.

From all the variety of shape and form experts divide chrysanthemums into different groups:

Greenhouse decoratives Very popular, with double flowers and incurving or reflexed florets ('petals'), or 'intermediates' midway between the two. A range of varieties will provide flowers from early autumn to mid-winter. Allow about six blooms per plant. Some favourites are: 'Balcombe Perfection', amber-bronze; 'Fred Shoesmith', white; 'Red Balcombe Perfection', bright red; and 'Yellow Fred Shoesmith', yellow.

Greenhouse incurved Much used for exhibition. Allow up to six blooms per plant. Ball-shaped blooms with incurving florets, produced in late autumn. Favourites include: 'John Hughes', white; 'Lilian Shoesmith', orange-bronze; 'Red Shirley Model', red and copper; and 'Yellow John Hughes', yellow.

Large exhibition Formerly known as Japanese. Huge blooms, much used for exhibition when only one or two blooms should be allowed on each plant. Flower in late autumn. Good varieties are: 'Cossack', crimson; 'Duke of Kent', white; 'Green Goddess', pale green; 'Harry Gee', silvery pink; 'Jessie Habgood', white; 'Shirley Primrose', pale yellow; and 'Yellow Duke', a deep yellow.

Single chrysanthemums Single daisy-like flowers. Can either be grown as sprays (remove the centre bud from each shoot) or disbudded to leave one flower per stem. Flower in late autumn and early winter.

Spray chrysanthemums Excellent for cutting. Masses of small flowers from mid-autumn until mid-winter. Single- and double-flowered and quill-petalled varieties are available.

Anemone-centred Small daisy-like flowers with cushion-like centres. Good for cutting. Come in a range of bright colours. Grown as for the singles.

Spider chrysanthemums Very popular for flower-arranging is 'Rayonnante' with long quilled florets. Colours include white, yellow, pink and bronze.

Charm chrysanthemums These make excellent pot plants, about 45 cm (18 in) in height and very bushy. They smother themselves with small single flowers, in a wide range of colours, from mid–autumn to early winter. Plants can be raised from seeds sown early in the year (mid–winter) in a minimum temperature of 10° C (50° F). They can also be grown from cuttings in the normal way. Pinch out tips of plants when 7.5 to 10 cm (3 to 4 in) tall and then allow to branch and grow naturally.

Cascades These are raised from seeds as for the Charms, or from cuttings. They make excellent pot plants and have a pendulous habit of growth, but the shoots need training to suitable supports to make them hang down. Pots of Cascades need to be raised on staging while growing and while flowering in the greenhouse. They produce small flowers in a wide range of colours.

If you try to economize when buying stock you may well be disappointed, so do spend the extra money on ensuring good quality. Throughout the year keep an eye on the plants and quell any disease as soon as it appears. Plan your chrysanthemum show from year to year. The best time to choose stock for taking cuttings is when the plants are in full flower but do not hesitate to reject any plants which have the slightest sign of distorted flowers, weak growth or mottled leaves.

To grow chrysanthemums in the greenhouse you will want to be able to keep the temperature at a minimum of 7 or 10° C (45 or 50° F) to get autumn and winter flowers. Good light is a must. To harden off your cuttings, a frame is a good idea but not essential.

THE GROWTH OF CUTTINGS

As they grow your chrysanthemum cuttings will produce several shoots but you can manipulate the plants to produce the kind of flowers you want. If you want several large single blooms on each plant completely remove the tops of the single stems when 15 cm (6 in) of growth has been achieved and the buds are beginning to break. Done carefully without bruising the plant, this will encourage side shoots to grow. After this you can take off all but the central bud on each side shoot.

The only chrysanthemums which do not need disbudding are the spray, single, anemone, Charm and Cascade varieties which, left untampered with, produce enormous numbers of small, starry blossoms.

There are three main methods of chrysanthemum-growing to choose from, each with its advantages, but the one you select will probably depend on the varieties you choose.

Left Freesias can be grown from seeds or corms and their deliciously scented blooms are produced in winter.

Right Melons are fairly simple to cultivate and the ripening fruits fill the greenhouse with a sweet, heady aroma.

POTS

In this method chrysanthemum cuttings are first rooted in boxes then transferred to 7.5 cm (3 in) pots, followed by 12.5 cm (5 in), then 20 cm (8 in) pots in which they mature and flower. The 12.5 cm (5 in) pots are best filled with John Innes No. 2 compost, but add plenty of crocks and a layer of rough fibrous material such as rough peat at the bottom of the pot to give good drainage. For the final potting in the largest-size pots, use John Innes No. 3 compost and an extra thick layer of roughage. The plants are stood outdoors for several months, from early summer to early autumn, then taken back into the greenhouse to flower. This leaves the greenhouse free during the summer for other crops like tomatoes.

To stop the larger plants from keeling over put three or four strong canes, each about 1.3 m (4 ft) long, round the edge of each pot and tie twine between them.

PLANTING

In the planting process, the chrysanthemum cuttings are first established in pots then planted in borders inside the greenhouse. The best time for planting is early to mid-autumn, well before the winter frosts set in. At this stage you will probably have the young plants in 12.5 or 20 cm (5 or 8 in) pots (for details see the previous section), or growing in good rich soil outdoors in a sheltered spot.

For good results it is worth the trouble of preparing the greenhouse thoroughly before putting the chrysanthemums inside. Fork over the soil in the borders and add 113 g (4 oz.) of a good general fertilizer to every m² (square yard). Using a spade and keeping as much soil as possible round the roots of each plant, plant the chrysanthemums in the border. Water them well. Over the next few days you may notice some wilting but the plants will recover quickly as long as you keep the greenhouse cool. After a couple of weeks heat the greenhouse to 7–10° C (45–50° F).

DIRECT PLANTING.

Though a great favourite with commercial chrysanthemum growers, direct planting is often a nuisance for amateurs because it takes up so much greenhouse space. This means that you will only be able to squeeze in an early crop of tomatoes. Because they develop much more quickly in the greenhouse there is no need to put in chrysanthemum plants until well into the summer. Choose your time, from early to late summer.

Another difficulty of direct planting is that it may be difficult to grow or obtain cuttings which are at the right stage of maturity. One good idea is to take cuttings early in the year, to establish them in the greenhouse, stop them when they are growing vigorously by pinching out the tops, then taking another set of cuttings and rooting those.

Chrysanthemums planted direct will be best if kept at a constant temperature of 13–15.5° C (55–60° F), especially when the buds are forming in early and mid-autumn and, of course, regularly fed and watered. When feeding concentrate particularly on nitrogen and potassium and ventilate well. Support the plants well and allow plenty of space – a minimum of 25 cm (10 in) – between each.

PROPAGATION

Plan your propagation programme well in advance so that you are ready to take cuttings at the right time of year. Take cuttings of large exhibition chrysanthemums in early and mid-winter and the rest in late winter or early spring.

Select your cuttings from plants which have spent the winter in a protected frame or frost-free greenhouse. From below a joint, take each cutting 5–7.5 cm (2–3 in) long. Always strip off the lower leaves, then dip the cuttings in hormone powder. For rooting make up a mixture of equal amounts of peat and sand and put in the cuttings 12–19 mm (½–¾ in) deep and 2.5–3.8 cm (1–1½ in) apart in seed trays. Water them well, then keep them at 13–15.5° C (55–60° F). Within a fortnight to a month the cuttings should have rooted – you can tell when rooting is well established because the tips of the cuttings become a fresh green – but you can help speed up the process by covering the box with a sheet of polythene to keep in air and moisture, or by using a proper propagating unit. One particularly good way of propagating chrysanthemums is to put the cuttings into peat pellets. Once cuttings have rooted transfer them to 7.5 cm (3 in) pots filled with John Innes potting compost No. 1 or some other good compost. Or you can plant them 12.5 cm (5 in) apart in a good rich soil in a cold frame.

GREENHOUSE CARNATIONS

As long as your greenhouse is light, airy, and can be heated to 4.5° C (40° F), it should be an excellent spot for growing carnations. There are hundreds of varieties to choose from, but the perpetual flowering Sim sports, which you can select from any good grower's catalogue, will give you the best results.

Buy young carnation plants early in the year and arrange for them to be delivered in mid-spring. At this stage they will be in 7.5 cm (3 in) pots ready for moving into 15 cm (6 in) pots with No. 3 John Innes compost or for planting out in beds.

When the plants are well established, take off the tips to encourage side shoots to grow. Regular watering is a must for carnations and an even temperature of 13–15.5° C (55–60° F) during summer. Always avoid sharp changes of heat which will damage the plants, and give them plenty of air. As the carnations get taller you wll need to support them with canes.

As soon as you have cut your first flowers you can begin feeding with a well-balanced fertilizer. To keep a regular supply of stock going, take cuttings in early and late spring. This will also mean that you have a good supply of plants to replace old ones which are becoming 'leggy' and that you can ward off rusts and the red spider which are the carnation's most fierce attackers. For cuttings choose shoots well above the base of the plant and just below the flowers. Root them in sand.

Recommended varieties

Name	Colour/Height
'Arthur Sim'	White, pencilled scarlet, T
'Dusty Sim'	Pastel pink, T
'Fragrant Ann'	Pure white, D
'Harvest Moon'	Golden-yellow, T
'Joker'	Crimson, M
'Lena'	Salmon pink, T
'Shocking Pink Sim'	Bright pink, T
'Skyliner'	Yellow, finely striped scarlet, M
'Tangerine Sim'	Tangerine, T
	T=tall M=medium D=dwarf

CHAPTER 8

GREENHOUSE FOOD CROPS

There are few more pleasurable sensations for a gardener than eating home-grown crops especially when those foods are out-of-season delicacies. Many fruits and vegetables are easy to grow in the greenhouse and need little attention apart from routine care. More important is knowing the particular demands of each plant and to plan your planting from season to season.

MELONS

Delicious to the taste buds, melons are fairly simple to cultivate. After you have finished your spring propagating programme a few melon plants can be put on a bench or in part of a border on the sunny side of your greenhouse.

Sow melon seeds in early or mid-spring. Use 7.5 cm (3 in) peat pots and put one seed in each by pressing it in sideways. Fill the pots with John Innes No. 1 or some other good compost. During the germination process – it will take about a month for seedlings to reach 15–20 cm (6–8 in) tall and be ready for planting out – you have plenty of time to prepare the permanent beds. To do this, mix a 60 cm (2 ft) mound of soil with about a fifth or a sixth of its bulk composed of well-rotted manure. For every bushel of the mixture add a 226 g (8 oz) dressing of tomato base fertilizer, that is, medium potash. Or you can simply use John Innes No. 2 potting compost. Alternatively plant in a growing bag, two plants per bag.

When the seedlings are growing strongly – in mid- or late spring – set the plants, still in their degradable peat pots, well up in the soil and give them plenty of warmth. This way they will get full light and have more resistance to disease. To encourage the side shoots to flourish pinch out the tip of the growing shoot. These laterals can then be carefully trained to horizontal wires or a light, temporary wooden framework, such as a section of trellis. There is no need to stick to a rigid pattern. Just train the plants in the most convenient way.

To get mature fruits you will need to pollinate the female melon flowers by hand. Strip off the male flowers and stroke them over the female flowers, or use a soft paintbrush to transfer the pollen. Although it is a wise precaution to pollinate all the female flowers, only let four fruits develop on each plant. As these get heavier support them with small string nets. They are easily made out of old netting.

From germination onwards melons need plenty of water, plus liquid feed, and especially when the fruit is swelling. Once the fruits are fully developed you can cut down on both. The fruit is ripe when the top responds to gentle pressure and when a sweet heady aroma fills the greenhouse.

These are some of the best varieties to choose from:

'Emerald Gem'	Green flesh, excellent flavour.
'Blenheim Orange'	Delicate flavour, rich scarlet flesh.
'Hero of Lockinge'	Early to mature. Prolific, white-fleshed fruits set freely.

CANTELOUPE MELONS
These delicious varieties can be raised in the greenhouse then transferred to a cold frame where they will mature and bear fruits:

'Charentais'	Early medium-sized fruit. Delicious flavour, deep orange flesh.
'Early Sweet'	Deep salmon flesh, very sweet.
'Ogen'	Early variety, small fruits, very sweet
'Sweetheart'	Medium fruits, light orange flesh.

CUCUMBERS

Like melons, their botanical relations, cucumbers are surprisingly simple to grow. There is no need to fill the greenhouse with them for half-a-dozen plants should supply all your salad needs Why not try growing early cucumbers then following these with mid-and late-season plants once your benches are free of spring cuttings?

Sow cucumber seeds from late winter onwards. Fill 7.5 or 10 cm (3 or 4 in) peat pots with John Innes No. 1 or some other good-quality alternative and press one seed sideways into each. With a temperature of 15.5–18° C (65–75° F) germination should take place within 48 hours. Discard any seedlings that come through later than this – they will lack vigour. When the plants are 15 or 20 cm (6 or 8 in) tall move them to 10 or 12.5 cm pots and support them with small canes.

A good way of growing cucumbers is to plant them on a ridge 60 cm (2 ft) high. If you do this mix equal parts of good loamy soil and well-rotted farmyard manure. John Innes potting compost No. 2 will give excellent results, too, but does tend to dry out rather quickly. Or plant cucumbers in growing bags. Before you set the plants out – they should be at least 60 cm (2 ft) apart – make sure that the soil and the air in the greenhouse are at around 18° C (65° F). Rather than carrying out elaborate schemes for training the developing plants simply train them up strings like tomato plants or tie them to horizontal wires, but if you choose the first method you will need to cut back some of the foliage.

Throughout their growing season cucumbers need plenty of water. They love a moist muggy atmosphere and this is easily created by frequent spraying, but this may not be possible if you have other crops to consider. During very hot weather you may need to shade the greenhouse glass and increase the ventilation. When the plant roots can be seen on the surface of the ridge, top dress them with a mixture of soil and farmyard manure. Unlike melons, cucumbers set their fruits without pollination, and in fact male flowers are best removed regularly for fertilized fruits have an unpleasant flavour. Many varieties today produce only female flowers, so there are no male flowers to remove. Other ways of growing cucumbers are in boxes or even very large pots containing a mixture of soil and manure.

Select your cucumbers from these successful varieties:

'Amslic'	Heavy cropper with female flowers only
'Brunex'	All-female variety, tolerates fluctuating temperatures
'Femspot'	Early maturing, all-female flowerer, needs plenty of heat
'Monique'	All-female flowerer, very heavy crops
'Pepinex 69'	All-female variety for cool or cold greenhouse
'Petita'	All-female for cool or warm greenhouses
'Sigmadew'	Suitable for cool or cold greenhouses

VINES

The only problem likely to thwart you if you plan to grow grapes in your greenhouse is lack of space, for while vines can be small and well controlled when young, they will eventually oust all the other plants from a small house.

The ideal way to plant vines is in a special border of rotted turves fortified with plenty of bone meal and sulphate of potash. But because the roots will take up a large area you may have to be content with planting the vines outside the greenhouse and leading the stems in through holes in the house just above ground level. As well as giving the roots a free run this system will be far less demanding on your water supplies.

Vine plants, which are usually called rods, are best planted in the greenhouse when two or three years old. If you are growing more than one, plant them at least 90 cm (3 ft) apart. All through the growing and fruiting season water them well and give balanced liquid feeds, especially when the fruits are swelling.By regulating the greenhouse temperature carefully you can pick early crops of grapes, but if you have the needs of other plants in mind a steady temperature will merely delay ripening and probably reduce the crop. Ideally you should start off with a temperature of 7° C (45° F) and raise this to 18 or 21° C (65 or 70° F) during the flowering season. After this an even temperature of 18° C (65° F) gives the best results.

To prevent stressing the vines do not pick the fruit of new rods for a year or two. It is best to take off the flowers in the first year. As the vine grows larger trim the growing tip to fit the greenhouse conveniently. Pruning a vine can be a tricky problem and it is worth giving the problem some forethought before you wield the secateurs. In early winter cut back half to two thirds of the season's growth on the main stem and trim the side shoots so that two or three plump buds remain – these buds can be easily noticed near the junction of the side shoot with the main stem. Every year allow two new side shoots or laterals to develop at each growing point to begin with but cut these back so that there is one lateral branching in each direction every 30 cm (12 in). Tie these established laterals securely to wires. When you have decided that the rods are old enough to bear fruits let the flower trusses form naturally then pinch off the leading shoot two leaves past the flowers. Once the fruits start to swell thin them drastically or you will have bunches of small dry bitter grapes. Vine scissors are the best implements to use. Aim for berries 2.5 cm (1in) apart within each truss.

Vine growing is often made to sound very complicated but the secret of success in a small greenhouse is undoubtedly rigorous pruning. The largest cut-back is best done in early winter, though mid-winter will do, followed by ruthless cutting throughout the growing season. Vines have remarkable powers of recuperation and rarely show signs of resenting such harsh treatment. A good variety of white grape is 'Buckland Sweetwater'; of black grape 'Black Hamburg'.

LETTUCE

Lettuce has a part in the plans of nearly every keen greenhouse gardener for it is the mainstay of salads, surprisingly hardy and quick to mature. Modern methods of plant breeding have produced a whole spectrum of varieties, some 'short day' which flourish in the dull days of winter, others 'long day' which do best in late spring through to mid-summer when sunlight is at a maximum.

A good planting plan to give you lettuce for six months of the year, before your outdoor crop is ready, is set out below:

SEED SOWING PERIOD	PLANTING IN GREENHOUSE OR FRAME	CUTTING	COMMENTS
Early autumn	Mid-autumn	Early winter	These are difficult crops for poor light areas
Late autumn	Early winter	Late winter/ early spring	
Early winter	Mid-winter	Early spring/mid-spring	
Mid-winter	Late winter	Mid-spring/late spring	
Late winter	Early spring	Late spring	

There are many ways of sowing lettuce seeds but the best way is to spread them thinly in boxes containing John Innes seed compost, U/C mix or peat compost. When they are large enough plant the seedlings out into well-dug borders dressed with general purpose fertilizer. Small varieties which will mature during winter can be planted 17 cm (7 in) apart, larger ones, and those needing more light, 20 cm (8 in) apart. Another popular planting method is to prick out seedlings into peat pots and then leave them to grow before they are finally planted out. Always insert the young plants into moist soil and keep them well watered. On no account wet the leaves. Water early in the day. It is important to choose the right varieties for your greenhouse. Some can be grown over winter without artificial heat, some need a cool greenhouse, and others will only succeed in an intermediate house.

The secret of successful lettuce growing is to give them a fast uninterrupted growing period from planting to cutting. The following varieties will give good results:

Lettuce varieties for the greenhouse:

'Columbus'   A fast grower with thick leaves for cold or cool greenhouse. Sow late sumer to late winter for harvesting in mid-autumn to late spring.

'Cynthia' A crisp good-flavoured lettuce for the cold or cool greenhouse. Sow late autumn to mid-winter for cropping between late winter and mid-spring.

'Dandie' A quick grower for the intermediate greenhouse. Sow late summer to late autumn for harvesting from late autumn to mid-spring .

'Kloek' Popular variety for unheated greenhouse. Sow late summer to mid-autumn for cutting between late autumn and early spring.

'Kwiek' Also very popular, a good lettuce for the unheated greenhouse. Sow late summer to early autumn for harvesting between late autumn and early winter.

'Marmer' A firm crispy lettuce for the cold or cool greenhouse. Sow late summer to mid-autumn to crop during late autumn/early winter; or sow in mid-late winter to cut during mid- to late spring.

'May Queen' A quick grower for the unheated greenhouse. Sow mid-autumn to late winter to crop between early and late spring.

'Noran' A good lettuce for the intermediate greenhouse. Sow late autumn to mid-winter to crop between early and late spring.

STRAWBERRIES

Although the forcing of strawberries is largely the province of the

Left For large bunches of good-sized grapes, the berries must be drastically thinned at an early stage. *Right* Grapes vines are vigorous and have to be kept in check by vigorous pruning in summer and winter.

professional greenhouse gardener there is nothing to stop a keen amateur from growing some strawberry plants, preferably in pots.

If you decide on strawberries as a greenhouse crop choose healthy one-year-old plants and, in late summer, pot them in 15 cm (6 in) pots containing John Innes No. 2 potting compost and stand them on a polythene sheet in a cold frame. Except during very severe weather these plants should need no protection until they are brought into the greenhouse in early or mid-winter.

In the greenhouse, give the strawberry plants a little water and moderate heat until they flower. At this stage they will need a temperature of 13–15.5° C (55–60° F). Most strawberries are self-fertile but you can dust the flowers with some cotton wool tied on a stick to ensure good pollination. Although the plants will need plenty of water try to keep the fruit dry as it swells by supporting it on straw or with wire. Depending on the variety and the temperature in your greenhouse, you should have fruit in mid- or late spring. Some good strawberry varieties are: 'Cambridge Vigour', 'Gorella', 'Grandee', 'Pantagruella', 'Redgauntlet', 'Rival' and 'Tamella'.

FRENCH BEANS

In a lean-to greenhouse climbing French beans are an ideal crop as there will be a large expanse of south-facing wall. Sow the seeds of these beans in early spring in peat pots, and plant them out into a well-dug and manured border during mid-spring, 30 cm (12 in) apart. To stop the stems bending and breaking support them with string or canes and, if necessary, trim them back. Give them plenty of water, warmth and a light spraying on the morning of a sunny day.

You can grow dwarf French beans in much the same way. Sow the seeds 4 or 5 to a 20 cm (8 in) pot or 5 or 6 to a 25 cm (10 in) pot. Half-fill each pot with John Innes potting compost No. 2. Add more compost when the plants are about 15 cm (6 in) high.

Good climbing varieties are 'Blue Lake', 'Garrafal Oro', 'Largo' and 'Purple Podded'. Recommended dwarf varieties are 'Sigmacropper', 'Sprite' and 'Tendergreen'.

PEACHES AND NECTARINES

Like vines, peaches and nectarines take up a lot of greenhouse space but are worth considering if these are your favourite fruits. A cool or unheated lean-to greenhouse is probably the easiest place to grow them as it has a ready-made wall.

A tree trained into a fan shape and two or three years old is the best starting point. Plant it in a well-drained loamy border and tie the branches to horizontal wires. Depending on the greenhouse temperature flowers should form in late winter or early spring and you can obtain good pollination with a soft paintbrush. As the fruits appear thin them out so that there is one for roughly every 30 cm² (sq ft) so that each is juicy and succulent. Plenty of water at the roots, plus daily spraying of the leaves during the morning are a must.

To train the branches of a peach or nectarine as they grow simply tie them to your system of horizontal wires. Ruthlessly remove all badly-placed growth, especially branches which grow outwards into the greenhouse. Every winter you will need to cut out old shoots that have carried fruits. Cut back to the new shoots that have formed. These will replace those you have removed and bear fruits the following summer.

Good peach varieties are 'Bellegarde', 'Dymond', 'Hale's Early', 'Peregrine' and 'Royal George'. Recommended nectarines are 'Early Rivers', 'Lord Napier' and 'Pine Apple'.

OTHER EARLY CROPS

ASPARAGUS
Lift well-developed plants into the greenhouse and pack them together under a 7.5 cm (3 in) layer of damp peat. Then place the whole under the greenhouse staging. With plenty of moisture plus darkness the shoots will quickly form.

RHUBARB
This is perhaps the easiest of all vegetables to force. In late autumn lift well-developed crowns. Let them become thoroughly frosted, trim the root ball, then pack them close together in peat. Put them under staging where they will be in complete darkness and water them heavily. According to the greenhouse temperature, pale pink shoots will form at a steady rate.

SEA KALE
In the autumn lift parent plants from your outdoor plot. Take off the side shoots and keep them for planting in the spring, then put the main plants in boxes or pots and cover them with 7.5 cm (3 in) of good humus-rich soil or old rotted manure. With heat, water and darkness succulent tender shoots will form in a few weeks.

CHAPTER 9

TOMATOES

Of all greenhouse plants tomatoes are the most popular. Any greenhouse will grow tomatoes as long as it gets good light and is reasonably warm. There is nothing quite like the first crop of your own tomatoes – they outclass any others for flavour and quality.

GROWING METHODS

There are several methods of tomato-growing to choose from. Select the one that suits your greenhouse and family appetites the best:

BORDER CULTURE
In this method tomato plants are grown in the border soil of the greenhouse. The greatest advantage of this is that it cuts down the amount of feeding and watering, but you will have to weigh this against the risk of soil deterioration caused by fungi, viruses and bacteria. In addition there may be a lethal build-up of plant poisons and fertilizer residues. Soil borders tend to be slow to warm up in spring and the plants difficult to control.

One way of getting round the disadvantage of border culture is to grow disease-resistant varieties of tomato and sterilize the border with a horticultural disinfectant each winter. But flood it with water to wash out any fertilizer residues, then allow it to partially dry out before sterilizing it.

RING CULTURE
This method involves growing plants in 22 cm (9 in) bituminized or plastic pots or rings on top of a 10–15 cm (4–6 in) layer of weathered ashes, gravel or some other inert material. The great advantage of ring culture is that you need little fresh soil each year. The plant growth is easy to control and the small amount of growing medium fully exposed to the heat. However the plants will need large amounts of water which is applied to the base layer, especially early in the year and you have to be careful not to upset their delicate nutritional needs. Feeds are applied to the rings.

LARGE POTS

Tomatoes will be happy in 25–30 cm (10–12 in) pots – plastic, clay or whalehide (bituminized paper). Use John Innes potting compost No. 2 or 3 (which can also be used for ring culture). Stand the pots on the greenhouse floor, 45 cm (18 in) apart each way, or on a soil border on a sheet of polythene.

GROWING BAGS

Probably the most popular method of growing tomatoes. The bags can be placed on the floor of the greenhouse or on a soil border. Most bags are 1.2 m (4 ft) long and will hold three plants comfortably. You need to support the plants in growing bags with special growing bag supports as canes cannot be used. Or you could support the plants with strings attached to the greenhouse structure.

SOWING AND PLANTING

Before beginning to plant tomatoes plan your moves carefully. Unless you have a really well-equipped greenhouse and excellent light avoid the earliest crops. Instead plant from early to mid-spring to get a good crop and to economize on heating costs.

SOWING DATE	PLANTING DATE	FIRST FRUITS RIPE
Late autumn	Late winter	Mid-spring
Early winter	Late winter	Mid- to late spring
Early to mid-winter	Early to mid-spring	Late spring
Late winter	Mid-spring	Early to mid-summer
Early spring	Mid-spring	Mid-summer

Sow your tomato seeds in trays or boxes and cover them lightly with compost. Water lightly and cover the seeds with a sheet of paper or paper and glass. The ideal germination temperature is 18° C (65° F). If it is higher than this you may get 'rogue' seedlings which produce no fruits when mature.

Three or four days after germination the seedlings will be big enough to handle and can be moved into 9 cm (3½ in) pots filled with John Innes No. 1 compost, the appropriate U/C mix or a peat compost. Keep young plants at 15.5–18° C (60–65° F) during the day, 13° C (55° F) at night, but lower this two or three degrees if the *day* has been dull. High daytime temperatures increase the growth rate but reduce the number of flowers on the bottom trusses and quicken ripening.

Keep the young plants well watered and if necessary give them a little high-potash liquid feed. When the first truss has at least one flower open they are ready for planting out. Waiting until this point is worthwhile as the fruit will set better.

Before planting out prepare your borders or rings. Dig the borders well and if you are using fresh soil add farmyard manure or garden compost. Next flood in lime by scattering it lightly then applying a fine mist from the hose; then, 10 or 12 days before planting add 170–212 g (6–8 oz) of tomato base fertilizer to every m² (square yard). This fertilizer, another John Innes standard, contaiins:

> two parts hoof and horn meal
> two parts superphosphate of lime
> one part sulphate of potash.

For ring culture and pots the best growing medium is John Innes potting compost No. 2 or 3.

Plant your tomatoes out 45 cm (18 in) apart, whether they are in borders, pots or rings. Make sure the soil is damp and use a trowel to dig the hole. Do not water in too well–add just enough liquid to wet the ball of roots.

HEAT, AIR AND WATER

The air temperature in the greenhouse at this stage should be about 18° C (65° F) by day and 13° C (55° F) by night. Obviously temperatures will vary but try to avoid very low daytime temperatures which will have a bad effect on fruit setting. The ventilators should be opened once the temperature reaches 21–23° C (70–74° F).

Tomatoes' water needs vary a great deal with the weather. For the first few weeks after planting out only water direct the roots of plants which wilt. A good daily spray with a fine rose will keep the atmosphere moist and encourage rooting, provided the temperature is around 18° C (65° F). For plants over 90 cm (3 ft) tall give the following amounts but take care not to overwater young plants as this may stunt them.

WEATHER	WATER/PLANT/24 HOURS
Cloudy and dull all day	0.14–0.28 litre (¼–½ pint) per plant
Overcast most of the time	0.28–0.42 litre (½–¾ pint) per plant
Cloudy, bright periods	0.71–0.84 litre (1¼–1½ pints) per plant
Occasional cloud, sunny	1.13–1.27 litres (2–2¼ pints) per plant
Very sunny, clear sky all day	1.7–1.84 litres (3–3¼ pints) per plant

FEEDING

Feeding can begin as soon as the first fruits start to form. Use a proprietary liquid tomato fertilizer according to the maker's instructions. Fertilizer can be applied once a week. For ring culture, apply the fertilizer only to the compost in the rings. Feeding can be gradually increased with advantage to once every five days for plants in rings, pots and growing bags.

Plants will need support almost at once. If possible make string loops and attach them to a wire 1.8 or 2.1 m (6 or 7 ft) above ground level or tie the plants to tall canes. Every morning or evening nip out any side shoots. As the plants grow carefully take off the bottom leaves to let the air circulate freely but *only* when they are yellow or diseased. If you have limited space pinch out the tops of the plants. To encourage surface roots to grow and to help keep the water in give the soil a top dressing of peat or thoroughly-rotted farmyard manure.

When pulling up tomato plants at the end of the season try to remove as much of the roots as possible. Burn the spent plants as far away from the greenhouse as possible and clean the house thoroughly to prevent diseases the next year.

Varieties to choose

'Ailsa Craig'	Well known, good-flavoured medium-sized fruits
'Alicante'	Very popular, early, with good-flavoured fruits
'Best of All'	Large fleshy fruits with few seeds
'Big Boy'	Extremely large fruits, ideal for slicing
'Dombello'	Very large meaty fruits of good flavour. Highly disease resistant
'Estrella'	Early, large firm fruits, highly disease resistant
'Eurocross A'	Early, excellent flavour and highly resistant to diseases
'Eurocross BB'	Early, ideal for short-day cropping, disease resistant
'Golden Boy'	Golden-yellow fruits, very sweet
'Golden Sunrise'	Yellow fruits of good flavour
'Grenadier'	Large fruits produced freely, disease resistant
'Harbinger'	Popular variety, early, with plenty of good-flavoured fruits
'Herald'	Early variety, vigorous grower, very sweet fruits, good disease resistance
'Ida'	Early, compact habit, medium-size fruits, highly disease resistant
'Moneymaker'	Highly popular variety bearing heavy crops of medium size fruits
'Odine'	Early, heavy cropping, round fruits, highly disease resistant
'Seville Cross'	Excellent early variety with good disease resistance, fruits of very high quality
'Shirley'	Early, heavy cropper, highly disease resistant

CHAPTER 10

PROPAGATION

Despite its technical sound the word propagation simply means raising new plants by sowing seeds, taking cuttings or dividing old plants. A greenhouse is far from essential for propagation but because its atmosphere is protected and controlled it will not only speed up the process but will give you a greater success rate and widen the range of plants that you can multiply to include a whole galaxy of tender and half-hardy species which need the warmth your greenhouse can offer.

Whatever the kind of propagation you have in mind you must be able to give newly-developing plants air, moisture and the right temperature. There is no infallible method which will bring success. Often trial and error is the quickest way of progress but there are some general rules which you should stick to.

SOWING SEEDS

Growing plants from seeds is cheap and gives good results but do reesist the temptation to collect your own from plants you have grown in the greenhouse. Rather buy from a reputable seedsman. The reason for this is that flowers which are fertilized with pollen from another plant may not breed true.

While some seeds, like those of the cucumber, germinate very quickly and easily, others, like primula seeds, are very difficult to germinate. One reason for this is a very hard seed coat which acts as a barrier and prevents water reaching the embryo within; another is that the seed may naturally have a long resting or dormancy period. For hard-coated seeds the best treatment is to soak them in tepid water before you sow them, as this will soften them and allow water in. To break the dormancy spell put the seeds into a refrigerator for a few weeks before taking them into a warm greenhouse.

The best substance to grow seeds in, whatever their size or shape, is U/C or John Innes seed compost, or some other all-peat mix. The container you choose will depend on how many seeds you plan to sow. For small batches use clay or plastic seed 'pans' or pots, for large ones seed trays are best. Available in plastic or polystyrene these trays have standard dimensions of 35 x 22 x 30 cm (14 x 9 x 12 in). Plastic seed trays are probably the best choice, as they are so simple to clean and are sometimes fitted with clear plastic 'domes' to make small propagating units.

If you are using a tray for sowing, fill the bottom with some roughage like rough peat before you add the compost. Clay pans and pots will need some pieces of crock put over the drainage holes. Other containers can be filled directly with the compost. Add it up to the rim, make sure it is warm and moist and press it down with a piece of wood so that the surface is even. Water well and allow it to drain, or stand the container in a shallow tray containing an inch or so of water for a few minutes.

The best way to sow fine seed is to scatter it thinly on the surface then press it in lightly. Hold the container at eye level to make sure of even sowing. Larger seeds can be scattered over the surface then covered with some more compost rubbed through a fine sieve. A method which has been tried and tested by gardeners for years is to put the seeds into a piece of cardboard folded down the middle. If you prefer to plant with finger and thumb, remember that fine seeds will stick to your fingers. Large seeds can merely be pressed into the compost.

Try to sow as thinly as you can and after sowing always give seeds a light watering with a very fine rose. Then cover them with a sheet of glass with paper on top. This keeps the humidity high and traps moisture. Light is unnecessary and often undesirable for germination. There is no need to cover with paper and glass if you are using an electrically heated propagating case. This will also provide a suitable germination temperature.

The ideal temperature for germination varies from species to species, but 18–21° C (65–70° F) will suit the majority. Look at the seed containers often to make sure they are not dry and turn the glass over every day so that drops of water do not soak the compost. As soon as you see signs of germination remove the paper and lift the glass a little to let some air in. Keep the seedlings out of bright sunlight, even if you have to protect them with a sheet of tissue paper.

VEGETATIVE PROPAGATION

As its name suggests, vegetative propagation involves taking off some part of the plant and inducing it to make roots. These cuttings may be from the stem, leaves or roots.

The most favourable time for taking cuttings is the season when the plant is growing most rapidly. For plants with soft stems, like dahlias and chrysanthemums, this will be early in the year when the new season's growth has begun. The cuttings do, however, need high temperatures between 15.5 and 18° C (60 and 65° F) to form roots.

Pelargoniums, hydrangeas and many other shrubs with more woody stems are best propagated later in the year. They can be rooted at lower temperatures, that is, from 10–13° C (50–55° F). Woody plants, like roses, give the best cuttings in autumn and will form roots at low temperatures but the vital rooting process will be speeded up considerably in the warmth of the greenhouse.

Usually the tips of side shoots, or sometimes the end of the main growing shoot, make the best cuttings, but do reject any plants which show signs of disease so that your cuttings are as healthy as possible. Use a very sharp knife or razor blade for taking cuttings.

The best length for a cutting is 5 or 7.5 cm (2 or 3 in) though some roses can be propagated from long cuttings bearing three or four buds. Whatever your plant make sure you do not bruise either parent or offspring during propagation. Put the cuttings in trays, seed pans or open beds which you have filled with rooting medium. This can be sand, peat, a mixture of the two, or one of peat and vermiculite. Or you can use peat pellets which do away with the need for transplanting later on. Make holes with a pencil and put the cuttings in 2.5–7.5 cm (1–3 in) apart having dusted them, if you wish, with hormone rooting powder according to the maker's directions.

Two common greenhouse plants, the rex begonias and saintpaulia, are often propagated by taking leaf cuttings. For the begonias take off a large leaf and make some cuts across the leaf veins on the underside then lay it on some rooting compost. Some gardeners put small stones over the cuts to hold the leaf in place. Take off saintpaulia leaves with a little of the stem attached and simply stand them in the compost. Both these sorts of leaf cuttings need high humidity.

All cuttings will make roots more quickly if you can set up some sort of humid, enclosed atmosphere. This may merely be a polythene bag held up with sticks, an electric propagating case or a mist propagating unit which carefully controls heat and moisture. Plastic propagating cases, consisting of a tray and a transparent cover are cheap to buy and very effective. A temperature of around 18° C (65° F) is needed to root cuttings.

PRICKING OFF AND POTTING

When seedlings are well grown and cuttings obviously rooting and established in the growing medium both can be transferred or pricked off into trays or pots of the right size. Do not choose pots that are too large. For most, 9 cm (3½ in) pots are ideal. And remember that plants in clay or plastic pots will need re-potting while those in peat or bituminized paper pots can be transplanted in their entirety.

To avoid damaging the leaves or roots gently tease seedlings out of their trays with a dibber. Look at the roots to make sure they are not diseased – they should be white, not brown – then make a hole in the new medium with your dibber and pop the seedling in. Then firm it with the dibber. If you are pricking off into standard trays put 8 seedlings per row in six rows and try to have some sort of grading system according to size. If you are using soil blocks you will have to add extra compost to fill up the indentation. Once they have been planted and firmed in give a good watering.

Cuttings can be handled very much like seedlings and both must be kept at a favourable temperature of around 15.5° C (60° F). Many gardeners think that in winter open benches give the plants a better start in life, but a closed-in situation will be better in summer as the plants will then need less watering.

The time for potting on or for planting out will depend on how quickly the new plants grow and how many roots they make. Moving a plant into a larger pot is quite simple. Choose a pot 5 cm (2 in) larger in diameter. Put a little roughage in the bottom and partly fill it with compost. Take the small pot containing the plant, turn it upside down and tap the rim lightly. Cup the ball of roots in your hand as the plant comes out so that it does not disintegrate, then put it on the compost layer in the new pot. Fill the pot to within 12 mm (½ in) of the rim and press in firmly if using soil-based John Innes compost, but only lightly if using peat-based compost.

All plants which will eventually flower or fruit outdoors must be gradually accustomed to temperatures outside the greenhouse. This hardening-off process is ideally accomplished in a cold frame, but a sunny sheltered spot will do. In a frame give more and more air each day until planting time in late spring when there is no chance of a late frost.

CHAPTER 11

DISEASES, PESTS AND OTHER PROBLEMS

In the congenial atmosphere of a greenhouse plants grow quickly but so too do all kinds of pests and diseases and the less the greenhouse environment is controlled the more rampant these pests and diseases will be. This, however, is not the whole answer and effective though modern chemical controls can be, many organisms have built up a resistance to these compounds.

Just as the human body is made more vulnerable by the extremes of cold and heat so greenhouse plants will be attacked more easily if you give them too much or too little food, excess or lack of water, if you overheat the greenhouse or forget to turn the heating on. Hygiene is important, too. Many pests and diseases are so small that they are invisible to the naked eye but regularly disinfecting your equipment will control them.

WARNING

If you use chemical pesticides *always* follow the manufacturer's instructions to the letter. Fumigants need particularly careful handling. *Lock all these substances away* out of the reach of children. All the chemicals mentioned in the following tables are easily obtainable from garden centres. The insecticides and fungicides are listed under their chemical names, rather than brand names. These will be found on all bottles or packs of pesticides (usually under the brand name).

Pests, Diseases and Problems

CROP, PLANT OR GREENHOUSE	DISORDERS	SYMPTOMS	PREVENTION AND CONTROL
General propagation, seed sowing, rooting cuttings, culture of young plants, bedding plants, etc.	Damping off: Pythium spp: Rhizoctonia Spp. Phytophthora spp	Base of seedlings and young plants turns light brown and stem constricts. Plant eventually collapses. Cuttings attacked in area of cut part or at compost level.	Cheshunt compound or liquid copper can be used before sowing and also for newly-germinated seedlings
General propagation, seed sowing, rooting cuttings, culture of young plants, bedding plants, etc.	Grey mould	Attacks cuttings or young plants. Starts as light brown lesion, eventually becoming covered with grey dust-like spores	Encouraged by high humidity. Especially troublesome in a greenhouse which is allowed to chill overnight. Use benomyl
Bulbs and corms; carnations, chrysanthemums, cucumbers, pot plants, tomatoes, lettuce, peaches, nectarines, and crops in general	Aphids of various species. Small flies can be seen on leaves, usually in clusters	Attack leaves, feeding on plant sap, causing distortion and loss of vigour Virus disease can also be transmitted by various species	Use insecticidal spray or atomizing fluid or smoke at first sign of attack, changing the nature of the chemical frequently, if possible, to avoid build up of resistance. Malathion, derris, gamma HCH, dimethoate, pirimicarb, permethrin are the main chemicals used.
Bulbs and corms; chrysanthemums, tomatoes, and several other crops	Caterpillars; Angle shade moth; Tomato moth	Caterpillars feeding on leaves and flowers, often at night	Gamma HCH smokes and sprays carbaryl, fenitrothion and trichlorphon sprays
Bulbs and corms; chrysanthemums	Stem eelworm (Ditylenchus dipsaci) attacks bulbs and other plants. Chrysanthemums attacked by specific eelworm (Aphelenchoides ritzema-bosi)	Attack leaves and flowers causing distortion. In chrysanthemums brown blotches are formed on leaves, changing from yellow to bronze and purple	Destroy stock of bulbs and use only fresh soil in future. Chrysanthemum stools can be hot water treated – 46°C (115°F) for 5 minutes

CROP, PLANT OR GREENHOUSE	DISORDERS	SYMPTOMS	PREVENTION AND CONTROL
Narcissus (daffodils)	Leaf scorch (Stagonospora curtisii)	Leaf tip turns reddish brown, followed by death	Spray with benomyl at first sign of attack and repeat several times
Bulbs and corms; Carnations, chrysanthemums, cucumbers, pot plants generally, tomatoes, indoor shrubs	Thrips of various species, small brown or yellowish insects	Attack plants in various ways – sucking sap from leaves or flowers, causing acute distortion of growth. Silvery spots often show, especially on carnations. Breeding is more or less continuous	HCH smoke varied with permethrin and pirimiphos-methyl applied repeatedly until control is gained
All crops	Grey mould (Botrytis cinerea)	Attacks a wide range of plants, causing discoloration of leaves, followed by grey dust-like mould. Spreads extremely rapidly. Tomatoes badly attacked on stems, leaves or fruit. Ghost spot on fruit is caused by partial development of botrytis. Lettuce can also be badly attacked	Keep atmosphere dry by skilful ventilation and application of heat. Avoid severe night temperature drops. Use benomyl (systemic) or tecnazene smoke
Carnations	Carnation fly	Eggs laid on upper surface of leaves, resulting in larvae which move into the stem	Gamma HCH smokes and sprays
Many crops and plants	Earwigs	Bite holes in flowers and stems during night, causing acute distortion and malformation	Trap with inverted pots, and spray or dust with gamma HCH
Many crops and plants	Red spider mite (Tetranychus urticae and T. cinnebarinus)	Nymphs and adults suck sap from leaves, causing yellowing and eventual destruction of leaves. Webs develop on underside of leaves, hindering control	Extremely persistent pests, over-wintering in cracks in greenhouse. A variety of materials should be used as smokes or sprays to avoid building up resistance. These include derris, malathion and dimethoate
Carnations, chrysanthemums, pot plants and shrubs	Powdery mildew (Oidium sp.)	Dirty white powder on leaves, stems and flowers	Benomyl spray or dust at first sign of attack
Chrysanthemums, pot plants, tomatoes	Leaf miner (Phytomyza and Liriomyza solani)	Eggs laid on leaves produce larvae which tunnel into leaves	Gamma HCH aerosol, gamma HCH smoke, when attack first noticed
Chrysanthemums, cucumbers, melons, pot plants, tomatoes	White fly (Trialeurodes vaporariorum)	Eggs laid on leaves, hatching into nymphs which suck sap and exude honeydew on which moulds develop. Growth is distorted. In pelargoniums leaf spot may be spread by this pest	A variety of sprays, dusts, aerosols, or smokes can be used, based on gamma HCH, malathion, pyrethrum, permethrin or derris. All must be used within 14 days and at short intervals to ensure control. Thoroughly clean or fumigate greenhouse in winter when empty

Pests, Diseases and Problems

CROP, PLANT OR GREENHOUSE	DISORDERS	SYMPTOMS	PREVENTION AND CONTROL
Cucumbers, melons, tomatoes	Leaf hoppers (Erythroneura pallidifrons)	Lively insects feeding on leaves cause distortion and restrict growth	Malathion at first sign of attack
Cucumber	Fungus gnats of various species	Develop initially on decaying fungi or FYM. Attack roots, causing wilting or death	Malathion watered into bed or use gamma HCH drench
Cucumbers, melons and other soft plants	Springtails of various species	White six-legged soil pests feeding on soft stems, roots and root hairs in clusters. Some actively jump by means of tails	Gamma HCH drenches or dusts
Cucumbers, melons, lettuce, tomatoes and practically all other plants	Symphylid (Scutigerella immaculata)	Very active 6 mm (¼ in) long insects feeding on roots, causing hard or deformed growth. They move down to lower depths of soil in winter or when soil is wet. Worst in highly organic soil	Throughly sterilize soil by heat or effective chemicals. Malathion drenches can be reasonably effective
Cucumbers, tomatoes and other plants	Woodlice of various species	Attack plant roots or stems at soil level with drastic effects if in large numbers	Bait with cut turnips. Gamma HCH
Cucumbers	Black rot (Microsphaerello citrullina)	Dieback of laterals at main stem. Identified by small black spots	Thiophanate-methyl spray, coupled with sterilization of boxes, etc. to avoid spread of infection
Lettuce and other crops	Leatherjackets, various species	Tough leathery looking grubs 12–25 mm (½–1 in) long, feed on roots	Gamma HCH or carbaryl dusts before planting. Can be very troublesome on new soils
Lettuce	Millepedes, various species	Many-legged 25 mm (1 in) long creatures attacking roots and stems	Normally feed on organic matter. Adequate soil sterilization with gamma HCH is most effective: or use carbaryl dust
Lettuce, pot plants	Downy mildew (Bremia lactucae and other species)	Yellow areas on upper surface of leaves with grey fungus on correspondingly lower areas	Benomyl at first sign of attack
Pot plants, peaches, nectarines, vines	Mealy bug (Pseudococcus spp.)	Little bugs covered with waxy secretion cluster on plants and cause distortion or loss of vigour, followed by leaf loss	Malathion sprays and dusts. Methylated spirit applied directly to vine stems or peach branches is also effective
Vines, cyclamen and other plants	Vine weevil (Otiorrhynchus sulcatus)	Eggs laid in soil hatch in 2–3 weeks and white grubs feed on roots, causing wilting	Add gamma HCH to compost if in doubt, or gamma HCH drench at first sign of attack

CROP, PLANT OR GREENHOUSE	DISORDERS	SYMPTOMS	PREVENTION AND CONTROL
Cyclamen	Root and tuber rots (Cylindrocarpon radicola and Thielviopsis basicoli)	Soil borne disease which attacks and rots tubers and roots of cyclamen	Use sterilized compost. Thiophanate-methyl drench is also effective
Tomatoes	Potato root eelworm (Heterodera rostochiensis)	Resting cysts start early in season releasing minute larvae which attack root systems, causing browning of lower leaves and wilting of plant. Their activities allow entry of root rots and other diseases	Very difficult to gain complete control in tomato borders. Alternative methods of cultivation allowing isolation from borders, using sterilized media, are advisable in bad cases
Tomatoes	Root-knot eelworm (Meliodogyne spp.)	Roots attacked, resulting in a deformed and galled appearance. Will rest in soil for 2 years in absence of host plants	Adopt alternative cultural methods
Tomatoes	Buckeye rot	Soil borne spores splash on to fruit causing disfiguring dark brown rings	Take great care when watering, avoid splashing. Adequate ventilation will also help. Spray with thiophanate-methyl at first sign of attack
Tomatoes	Didymella stem rot (Didymella lycopersici)	Attacks plants at soil level, causing brown-grey sunken lesions which extend up the stem, eventually girdling it, killing plants. Shiny spores may be seen on detailed examination with a lens	Sterilize house thoroughly in winter and get rid of infected haulms well away from greenhouse. Sterilize soil thoroughly by heat
Tomatoes	Leaf mould (Cladosporium fulvum)	Starts as yellow spots on upper surface, with corresponding grey-brown mould patches on lower surfaces. Appearance of disease coincides with periods of still muggy weather, when humidity is high. Once established it can spread rapidly and affect flowers as well as leaves. Has an overall yield-reducing effect	Certain districts are notorious for this disease, especially those where humidity is high. It is always advisable to grow resistant varieties in bad areas. When non-resistant varieties are grown, spray with copper in season. Good ventilation night and day, coupled with adequate air movement by means of fans or use of heaters, will do much to offset the trouble

PHYSIOLOGICAL DISORDERS

Tomatoes	Blossom end rot	This is caused by inadequate or irregular watering or too high a salt content
	Cracking or splitting of fruit	Due to widely varying environmental conditions and may largely be influenced by type of weather
	Dry set and blossom drop	Due again to irregular growing conditions, especially temperatures below 18° C (65° F) and above 27° C (80° F) also perhaps to virus infection
	Blotchy ripening	Caused by day temperatures being too high and by irregular feeding. Go on to regular liquid feeds and keep potash level high
Pot Plants	Over-watering	Always ensure by constant supervision that plants are not over-watered. Sometimes low night temperature has the same effect
Many Plants	Over-feeding	Apply less fertilizer or in more diluted form
	Lack of light	Make sure that plants obtain maximum light, especially in winter, bearing in mind their likes and dislikes in this direction

Irregular ripening of fruit

Yellowing and wilting of lower leaves

Scorched appearance of foliage and leaf tips

Gross lanky growth

INDEX